# Shadow and Substance

## The Tabernacle of the Human Heart

David Laeger

Crest Books
The Salvation Army National Publications

Published by Crest Books,
Salvation Army National Publications
615 Slaters Lane, Alexandria, Virginia 22314
www.salvationarmyusa.org

Printed in Canada

Artwork and photographs courtesy of the Mennonite Information Center, 2209 Millstream Road, Lancaster, PA 17602 and Imperial Graphics, Leola, PA 17540

Book design by Laura Ezzell

Library of Congress Card Catalog Number: 2004116701

ISBN: 0-9740940-4-8

Shadow and Substance

# Dedication

To Lt. Colonel Edward Laity (the father of Lt. Colonel W. Edward Laity, an able student
of the Word), who impressed me deeply with lingering thoughts about the Tabernacle and
its teaching concerning Christ, when I was a cadet.

# Acknowledgments

Lt. Colonel Marlene Chase, who amidst the weight of so much else as National Literary Secretary and Editor in Chief, gave time
and expertise in the lengthy process of overseeing the book's production.

Colonel Henry Gariepy and Carolyn J. R. Bailey, who took diligence and time to read through the manuscript, giving from their
varied perspectives and suggestions for its printing.

Jeff McDonald, for the laborious task of refining the grammar, ensuring logical flow and readability of the text.

The Salvation Army National Publications (Crest Books) for acceptance and implementation of the manuscript.

My wife, Anna, who read through some of the manuscript as it was being written,
encouraging me with her own responses to its content.

The leading of the Lord, entrusting me with His marvelous truths, so much so that I am left with the sense that He still takes the
lowly things to confound the wise and strong. I know my tremendous limitations and unworthiness. To God alone be the glory.

# Table of Contents

The two followers of Jesus were restrained from recognizing the stranger who joined them as they trod dejectedly down the Emmaus Road (Luke 24:13-35). Mark writes in his Gospel that the stranger appeared "in another form." This is to say, "in a form of a different kind." It was not that Jesus' nature was changed, only His appearance as He approached them. However, He became progressively familiar to them, until, at last, the form by which they had known Him before was fully revealed—during the cool dusk of an evening meal.

Through His human nature Jesus Christ demonstrated His human heart.

> "Let this mind be in you which was also in Christ Jesus, who, being in the form of God, did not consider it robbery to be equal with God, but made Himself of no reputation, taking the form of a bondservant, and coming in the likeness of men" (Philippians 2:5-7).

Jesus was among them to work as a servant. Through His human nature He demonstrated His human heart. No creature has ever seen God's pure divine essence. But God does reveal Himself in a form by which His creatures can recognize Him as God: "For this man [Jesus] became flesh."

God needs no grounding in any one realm of existence. He is Spirit, and as such everywhere present, unconstricted by the need for form. But to appear in the realm of earthly existence, He would need to manifest His human nature through some visible form. He graciously chose the form of a servant. But when we see Him one day, we will see Him in His Sovereign Form!

When He stood on the Mount of Olives with Moses and Elijah to discuss the purpose for taking on the form of a man, "He was transformed before [the disciples]. His face shone like the sun, and His clothes became as white as the light" (Mark 9:2-3).

He was "metamorphosized." Nonetheless, His nature did not change—He was still God, and He was still man. Metamorphosis did not alter His nature, only His appearance. Following Him, we also are changed. Still, we will always be essentially human. We are immortally human, though our resurrection form will manifest itself in accord with our new-found existence and redeemed environment.

In thinking about the form of our lives and the form God chose to make Himself known, prophetic words by Paul add a sense of urgency to our investigation of the shadow and depth of Truth. Writing about the condition of the Church in the last days, Paul said that there would be those among us "having a form of godliness but denying its power" (2 Timothy 3:5).

How strange! An exterior appearance without an inward essence! A ritual without reality. A Tabernacle marked "Ichabod" (see 1 Samuel 4:21). An assembly without evidence of divine purpose—or presence.

This book examines the ancient Tabernacle and attempts to uncover not only God's nature but the implications of God's essence for the soul. Every effort has been taken to stay within the bounds of Scriptural truth. I have avoided speculating on meanings beyond what is taught in the Bible's own words, and have followed the principle of interpreting Scripture by Scripture.

The two sections of this book are meant to enable us to know the roots of our faith, the pattern of our formation (as it should be), and the content of our worship and service to God. The Old Testament Tabernacle symbolically gave us the pattern and formation; the New Testament uses the forms of the Tabernacle from the Old as a blueprint for the Church, the Living Tabernacle of God. And may He who is the Oracle, the Word of God, Jesus, find us fit to serve as His instruments of love and work. May the time come for the world to see that we are truly one Tabernacle, board joined to board, cloth to cloth, metal to metal, all refined, all pure, all orderly, all related by the work of the Holy Spirit, the will of the Father, by the reconciliation of the Son of God.

May the Lord grace this study of that ancient holy habitation with the truth that He intends His people to glean from it. May He guard us from tendencies toward extremes that might confuse or obfuscate more than edify. Amen.

# The Shadow of the Tabernacle

Through His human nature Jesus Christ demonstrated His human heart.

Jesus spoke of His own body as a "temple." Even as He became an increasingly controversial character in the eyes of priests in authority, He predicted His own fate by declaring, "Destroy this temple, and in three days I will raise it up ... But He was speaking of the temple [this sanctuary] of His body" (John 2:19,21).

Two Greek words found in the New Testament, *hieron* and *naos*, are generally translated simply as "temple." But there is a distinction. The first designates the whole temple complex, an engineering feat of enormous size and wonder, a complex of courts, colonnades, stairs, arches, and rooms, built upon a Jerusalem hill. Highly visible from a distance, the sight of it enraptured both friend and enemy. The public was allowed entrance to much of that area, and Jesus taught in some of those places. But only a select group could enter the central structure, the building called "the naos." These were the priests from the tribe of Levi, of the family of Aaron. Even Jesus of Nazareth was not sanctioned to enter that building. Hebrews 7:14 teaches, "For it is evident that our Lord arose from Judah, of which tribe Moses spoke nothing concerning priesthood." Hebrews 9:24 says, "For Christ has not entered the holy places made with hands, which are copies of the true, but into heaven itself, now to appear in the presence of God for us."

We find a remarkable revelation from the lips of Jesus: that His body mystically incorporates all that one would find in the Jerusalem sanctuary. The Lord spoke through the prophet Isaiah about this, saying, "The Lord of Hosts ... He will be a sanctuary" (Isaiah 8:13, 14). It is the same goal God was looking forward to when He gave instructions for the design of the original holy Temple, which was to be the Lord's dwelling place: "And let them make Me a sanctuary, that I many dwell among them" (Exodus 25:8).

In Psalm 27:4, David conveys the same meaning: "One thing I have desired of the Lord, that will I seek: that I may dwell in the house of the Lord all the days of my life, to behold the beauty of the Lord, and to inquire in His temple."

David was referring particularly to the larger of those two rooms that comprised the holy places, the *hekhal* (temple)—the Holy Place which was furnished with objects of worship. David, who was of the tribe of Judah, knew what was there, even though he was not a priest. His "desire" was more than an emotional feeling—it was a searching petition. He beautifully phrases his psalm to say, in essence, "I have inquired ... to inquire." Like a child who gains his father's attention only to seek more of it, David would fix himself within the confines of the Tabernacle to search for unconfined beauty and truth.

The Song of Solomon, in its highest intent, speaks of Jesus, romantically whispering, "He is altogether lovely" (Song 5:16). Psalm 45:2 prophetically asserts His incarnate perfection, His princely appearance as "fairer than the sons of men." And Horace Bushnell, in his book *The Character of Jesus*, writes with admiration, "His soul was filled with internal beauty and purity, having no spot or stain, distorted by no obliquity of view or feeling, lapsing, therefore, into no eccentricity or deformity." John in the prologue to his Gospel presents Jesus as the Eternal Word who sets up His humanity among us (1:14). The verb for "dwell" here is *skenoo*, which connotes the act of setting up a tent. The Apostle Paul refers to his own experience with Jesus as that of a tent spreading over him: "Therefore most gladly I will rather boast in my infirmities, that the power of Christ may rest upon me." The word is the same, though translated in 2 Corinthians 12:9 as "rest upon." If we sought the Lord as David sought Him, if we knew Him as Paul knew Him, we too would declare in speechless contemplation, "in Him dwells all the fullness of the Godhead bodily" (Colossians 2:9 NKJV).

Great would be our hesitations in the mention of His name. Our attempts to describe Him would evoke John Milton's question, "May I express Thee unblamed?" We would tremble upon the illumination granted, like the ancient saints. Yet He invites us into Himself, wherein is discovered that He also imparts Himself to our soul. We become—that is the best word we can use—we become, in our finite measure, as He is: a living Tabernacle. What we find in Him reflects its likeness in us.

For the sake of His own designs, let us discover freely the Christ Form of that ancient Tabernacle. For from that study, who He is and what He has done will become clearer and more real.

In the personal "temple" of Jesus, "dwells all the fullness of the Godhead bodily ..." (Colossians 2:9)

If you could have asked the prophets of the Old Testament to explain what they wrote, they would have replied that what they spoke and wrote excels human imagination and understanding. Peter, with the advantage of hindsight, explained it better: "The prophets diligently studied and searched out the coming grace revealed to them by the Spirit of Christ who was witnessing in them, inquiring about the time and manner of His passion and following glory." If these ancient prophets were kept from understanding divine mysteries, who else among men could grasp the Divine's reach into our world? Isaiah asked as much: "Is there anyone capable of believing what we prophesy?"

The holiest place of all in ancient Israel/Judah was in the Holy of Holies. There, on Yom Kippur, the Day of Atonement, the most serious of transactions in creation took place. The high priest performed his annual expiation for the sins of the nation.

Once a year blood was brought into the oracle, the Holy of Holies—also known as The Most Holy Place of the Tabernacle, the second and forbidden room, the dwelling place of God, the abode of the Shekinah Glory, the Holy Place of the Holy Ones. (The plural "holies" accords with some of the other names used in Old Testament references to deity. "Elohim" and "Yahweh" are plural names, used always with a verb in singular form, implying more than One Divine Person being and doing together. We believe, by New Testament revelation, that those names teach of the Trinity.)

Isaiah, interpreting the ritual of the high priest bringing sacrificial blood into the Tabernacle's oracle, prophesied of Christ, the Living Oracle, entering into the tabernacle of our blood (see Hebrews 2:14-18). The prophet himself could not explain it, but he knew of that One who alone would come to disclose those things. The Apostle Paul writes that in the personal "temple"of Jesus "dwells all the fullness of the Godhead bodily ..." (Colossians 2:9). Watch carefully the steps of Jesus' life, and it becomes clear that He and God are there, together. He is the Anointed One, filled and empowered thoroughly, perpetually, with the Holy Spirit (Luke 4:1,14), always in guided fellowship with His Father (John 5:17, 19, 20, 30; 8:16, 58; 10:30). Wherever He is, there is also the "Holy Place of the Holy Ones." It is to that final manifestation that the ancient Tabernacle testified so wonderfully.

Paul also takes the idea of "Tabernacle" as found in the Old Testament and sees in its form a foreshadowing of the Church.

> "... Christ—from whom the whole body [the Church], joined and knit together by what every joint supplies, according to the effective working by which every part does its share, causes growth of the body for the edifying of itself in love" (Ephesians 4:15,16).

The original Temple was carried by the Hebrews as they wandered in the wilderness in search of the promised land. They assembled and disassembled it as they journeyed. So it is with the Church. Whether together or apart in a physical sense, the members of the Church are united in a spiritual sense by holiness and love. Paul further admonishes that the Church is a Temple in which dwells the Holy Spirit (1 Corinthians 3:16); and that each member is a Temple of the Holy Spirit (1 Corinthians 6:19).

Shadow and Substance

Some might doubt Paul's extrapolating. They might ask, "Is it true? Where's the evidence?" Answers are found in the cross of Jesus. All that God accomplished there bountifully avails to make the Temple/Tabernacle completely holy: "Now may the God of peace Himself sanctify you completely; and may your whole spirit, soul, and body be preserved blameless at the coming of our Lord Jesus Christ" (1 Thessalonians 5:23).

And if we are such a temple, the reality of the furnishings found in the first Tabernacle will develop, in each of us, the Church of the Lord Jesus Christ.

## The Ark of the Testimony

The whole purpose of Israel's elaborate center of worship served to foreshadow Christ's life and work. Entering the interior of the Tabernacle, you would find the Tent housing two sacred rooms. The innermost room was the forbidden room, the Oracle, the room of divine secrecy, the Most Holy Sanctuary. It illustrates by its design and content the mind of God. It reveals His manner of reasoning, and by that reveals His nature, for as He is, He thinks. No words of God could ever contradict His own nature.

The purpose of this room is oracular. It is the place where God speaks. He communicates verbally, covenantally, and symbolically. Verbally, because it is where He spoke to Moses. Covenantally, because there the fundamentals of God's law for His people were kept. Symbolically, for its dimensions, objects, and materials typified heavenly realities and earthly necessities.

The Holy of Holies was a cube–shaped room. The side and back walls were made of acacia wood, overlaid with gold, held in place by silver sockets at the base. To stand within its space was to behold on three sides of the room a mirror of a perfect enclosure. Its fourth wall was a veil stretched from side to side, separating it from the first room. The veil was a beautiful work of colored cloth, embroidered with cherubic figures. The ceiling consisted of fine white linen, also embroidered with cherubim. It replicated in miniature the heavenly dwelling of God. It also demonstrated God's condescension to be with the creature He loves, made in His likeness, and how He desires to restore the image of that creature so marred by sin.

Some might conclude that a high, holy, lofty God simply cannot look upon sin. While He would no doubt prefer not to look upon it, He does see sin—God is not blind. Only because He saw our sinfulness did the creation of the Tabernacle and all the glory it implies become reality. His great heart of love moved Him to redeem us from sin's consequences. Of course, we wonder at His criss-crossing moves through history to chart His plan for redemption. Those moves seem slow, but they are diligently compassionate. Such is the importance of His ability to foreknow and foreordain that He will only and always do what is right, view His creation mercifully, and humbly walk us through His plans for our union with Him.

In the center of that room stood the Ark of the Covenant. Three memorial objects lay within it, each one representing something of God's nature and work: the stone tablets engraved with the Ten Commandments, Aaron's budding rod, and the manna. The Ark itself foreshadowed the actual presence of Christ, the Immanuel of Isaiah 7:14; those items in the Ark embodied qualities of Jesus' personhood as the Messiah, Yeshua, in relation to the world He came to save from sin (Isaiah 49:6,8). The material used to make the Ark conveyed the idea of God incarnate—pure gold for His Godhood, strong acacia wood for His durable manhood.

The Ark of the Covenant presents to us a portrait of the ultimate meeting place between God and humanity—for reconciliation. It speaks of what is found in Christ once restoration has taken place: righteousness, life, victories over death, and the sign of one's divinely appointed task.

"I am the Lord your God, who brought you out of Egypt, out of the land of slavery. You shall have no other gods before Me" (Exodus 20:1–7).

The stone tablets engraved with the Ten Commandments speak of victories over death. Though for the most part the commands speak in negative terms, they have a positive intention. They negate our sinful tendencies. They reveal how a life determined by sin is counter to the life determined by God. We are like the Hebrews in that we might have practiced negative things in ignorance, but after hearing the commandments see them to be offensive to God. These tablets carved by God and delivered to Moses to share with the people waiting at the bottom of Mount Sinai show that God speaks to us where we are to teach us the acceptable way to live.

The commands are divisible into two parts. One part outlines our relationship to God. The other outlines relationships to persons.

The law emerged out of God's love, just as the essence of our original human nature emerged out of Adam and Eve, before the Fall. God shows in His commands that He is like a loving parent, warning of consequences to disobedience. To adhere to His admonitions is to find the favor of His love.

Interestingly, the Law begins with something sin makes possible—the thought of having another god. The second command continues by warning against tangible aberrations of God. And the last command also confronts fallen thought—the thought of coveting what belongs to your neighbor. All of these are forbidden, and lead to activity addressed in the other negative commands. Jesus puts the commands in a positive light by summarizing them as: "Love the Lord your God with all your heart and with all your soul and with all your mind ... Love your neighbor as yourself" (Matthew 22:37,39).

1. Acknowledge no other god, for there is none other. Think only about the true God.
2. Form no other god, because the living God is beyond such forms, thus incomprehensible.
3. Do not use God's name without purpose, for His name is holy, and it speaks of His nature.
4. Remember the Sabbath to keep it sanctified, and you will find rest to your soul as you ponder and worship your Creator.
5. Honor your parents, for they are your procreators. To honor them honors God who chose them as instruments through which He gave you life.
6. You shall not murder. God is the Source of life and every soul is precious to Him, every term of life lies only within His authority, therefore reverence every human life.
7. You shall not adulterate. Adultery, by act or thought, distorts that likeness to God so beautifully made by the union of one man to one woman.
8. You shall not steal. Be satisfied with what you have and respect what belongs to another. Know your limits in the use of property not your own.
9. You shall not lie. Tell the truth or say nothing. Do not spread an evil report by assuming you know all the facts. Lying fails, but truth endures forever.
10. Do not covet, for even the thought of wanting what belongs to someone else opens the door to the commission of other sins—a covetous man will do anything to get what he wants.

Moses had received these commands twice, twice written on stone. The first tablets he broke in anger when he saw the licentious behavior of his people (Exodus 32). After the rage and the intercession of Moses, the Lord wrote His law afresh on two new stones.

When Jesus dealt with the adulterous woman and the hypocrites who condemned her, He may have called to mind that historical event when God rewrote the ten laws. Jesus stooped down to write, twice, in the sand, and whatever He wrote brought to each one present conviction for sin against divine law (John 8:1-12). Rabbi Jesus pierced their consciences with something that spoke of their common guilt. Perhaps He caused them to reflect upon personal, secret law–breaking thoughts and acts.

## Immutable Law

That these ten laws were written on something as impermeable and strong as stone implies that they are immutable. That God wrote them twice indicates that our breaking them does not change them. His laws are non–negotiable. Grey areas are finite problems. Absolutes are God's work. These ten absolutes shed light upon the character of God. He is perfectly righteous, entirely holy. They also disclose our marred image, and teach what it takes to resemble Him.

## Restored Image

In describing Jesus Christ as God's Son and Co–Creator, the author of the New Testament book of Hebrews employs a unique phrase.

"God ... has in these last days spoken to us by His Son ... being the brightness of His glory and *the express image of His person*" (Hebrews 1:1-3).

While every phrase in these verses provides a well for thought, the final one particularly relates to the subject at hand: "the express image of [the Father's] Person." The term for "express" is *charakter* in Greek, a name used for a dye tool engravers use to etch pliable surfaces. Out of extreme mercy, God re–introduced His personal nature, the nature He used to create the world and to transcribe laws on two engraved stones. He did so to teach us what is required to return to His original design for us. The first recipients of those laws found that restoration impossible.

Jesus' eternal nature, and His role as the creative essence through which the Father made the world and engraved the commandments, are described as the dye of God's character. To look inside the Ark of the Covenant is to get a glimpse of God's character and the restoration to come.

## Shiloh

Jesus is the Law–Giver, the One of whom Jacob prophesied in Genesis 49:10, calling Him "Shiloh": "The scepter shall not depart from Judah, nor a lawgiver from between His feet, until Shiloh come; and to Him shall be the obedience of the people."

The meaning of the name Shiloh is not clear, but it refers to Messiah. The One named is the same Person who came to Moses at Sinai as the engraver of the Law; He came again as the living embodiment of His Law; and He will return to judge perfectly all mankind, according to that Law. His life manifests law. His love works by law. Nothing He does contradicts His law.

You could say "It is set in stone!" Now it is to be written on the hearts and minds of His people, in the sanctuary of the human heart.

> "'The time is coming,' declares the Lord, 'when I will make a new covenant with the house of Israel and with the house of Judah. It will not be like the covenant I made with their forefathers when I took them by the hand to lead them out of Egypt, because they broke my covenant, though I was a husband to them,' declares the Lord.
>
> "'This is the covenant I will make with the house of Israel after that time,' declares the Lord. 'I will put My law in their minds and write it on their hearts. I will be their God, and they will be My people'" (Jeremiah 31:31-33).

The Stone Tablets of
the Law

# The Bowl of Wilderness Manna

From the beginning of their deliverance from slavery in Egypt, the Israelites witnessed amazing miracles. God's intervention claimed their memory forever. One of those miracles was the daily provision of bread from heaven, called "manna." To memorialize it, a bowl of manna was preserved in the Ark of the Covenant. It is associated with the Ark because God's covenant with His people included promised sustenance of the nation.

"He humbled you, causing you to hunger and then feeding you with manna, which neither you nor your fathers had known, to teach you that man does not live on bread alone but on every word that comes from the mouth of the Lord" (Deuteronomy 8:3).

## Manna and Showbread

Another kind of bread was also placed in the Tabernacle. This was bread of the earth, grain processed into unleavened loaves to become sacred food for the priests. The "showbread" was replaced weekly in the anterior room on a gold overlay table. Both the manna and the showbread symbolize something about Christ our Savior. The manna depicts His descent from heaven; the showbread portrays His human life, like grain, dying and rising again as a completed and abundant offering to God for His people. Both reveal the gift of God's Son for the nourishment of those who partake of Him: "But here is the bread that comes down from heaven, which a man may eat and not die. I am the living bread ... this bread is My flesh, which I will give for the life of this world. ... Whoever eats My flesh and drinks My blood has eternal life, and I will raise him up at the last day" (John 6:50-54).

As a memorial in the Ark of the Covenant, the manna and showbread relate to the Lord's selfless nature, to His desire to give. He not only gives loving commands, He increases our capacity to keep them. His commands imply His nature. His bread imparts His nature.

## Bread of Heaven

Jesus taught that He was the substance that manna only foreshadowed. He is the "Bread of Heaven." Through His flesh, i.e., His full humanity, comes the source of our eternal life.

"I am the living bread which came down from heaven ... and the bread that I shall give is My flesh ... Whoever eats My flesh and drinks My blood has eternal life ... It is the Spirit who gives life; the flesh profits nothing. The words that I speak to you are spirit and they are life" (John 6:51,54,63).

## Future Manna

The ramifications of manna understood in this way include a promise for the future. As Jesus makes clear to Christians of the church in Pergamos, Asia Minor, whom He addresses in Revelation 2:12-17, He promises to give "hidden manna" to those who overcome false doctrine, idol defilement, and sexual immorality. Just as the hidden manna in the Ark represented God's infinite presence with His people, so Jesus' reference to it means that whoever overcomes the evils of this world will enjoy the deep and secret communion of God forever.

## Present Manna

Until Jesus returns in glory, our manna is chiefly spiritual. That is not to say that this manna of Christ is some mere mystical experience—though certainly, our spiritual nature is first affected by it; then it permeates all of life. Nor does this point to the spiritual nourishment of the Lord's Supper. Manna is not a part of the Lord's Supper, but it implies "communion"—spiritual communion with our Savior, daily. This manna for today is daily fellowship with God. This spiritual manna, ingested through the week, prepares individuals for the *koinonia* (bonding) of the assembled members of the Church.

> "So they gathered it every morning, every man according to his need ... And so it was, on the sixth day, that they gathered twice as much bread ... Six days you shall gather it, but on the seventh day, the Sabbath, there will be none" (Exodus 16:21,22,26).

Ideally, every believer "gathers twice as much" in his daily communion with God, in anticipation of the Sabbath gathering. Such preparation and anticipation verifies what we mean by "church."

## Manna and Dew

"And when the dew fell on the camp in the night, the manna fell on it" (Numbers 11:9). The Lord does wondrous things while we sleep, or when dark trial envelopes. Jesus said that the Father is always working, and that He, Jesus, also is always working (John 5:17). Isaiah affirms the truth of God's continual industry:

"Have you not known? Have you not heard? The everlasting God, the Lord, the Creator of the ends of the earth, neither faints nor is weary. His understanding is unsearchable" (Isaiah 40:28).

"Behold, He who keeps Israel, shall neither slumber nor sleep" (Psalm 121:4)

The experience of devotion is only understood fully when we see that as we direct our attention to God, God also works in us. In personal prayer, morning by morning, the dew of the Holy Spirit falls upon the ground of the believing heart and nourishes with the likeness of the holy Son. And He never fails with His supply.

## Manna's Description

"Now the manna was like coriander seed, and its color like the color of bdellium ... and its taste like the taste of pastry prepared with oil" (Numbers 11:7,8).

Every item in the Tabernacle affects one or more of the human senses. Manna was like coriander seed, probably referring to its size, and affected the sense of touch. "Bdellium" refers to its color, probably (because the word is not firmly understood) something like white crystal. It also affected the sight. It was cooked in varied ways, no doubt affecting the sense of smell.

Manna tasted "like pastry prepared with oil." It had a brightness to it after falling to the desert floor as darkness gave way to dawn. It fell in abundance to the Israelites and its size was such that they had no problem finding it. As for its taste, its sweetness left a pleasant satisfaction.

As manna represents Jesus the Life–Giver, so communion with Him affects the inward person as well as the outward person. It was preserved within the Ark as a part of the Old Covenant, as a memorial of God's unceasing care and willingness to join us. Its spiritual counterpart is preserved by and in its Source and Guardian, the Lord Jesus Christ.

The Bowl of
Wilderness Manna

"Isn't it enough for you that the God of Israel has ... brought you near Himself to do the work at the Lord's tabernacle ... now you are trying to get the priesthood too" (Numbers 16:9,10).

How do you know which persons God has chosen for spiritual leadership? Aaron, Moses' older brother, was chosen by the Lord and publicly verified as the high priest of Israel. It proved to be an enviable position, for the esteem and notoriety it brought. The splendid uniform the high priest alone wore set him apart as one above others. No Israelite had grounds for seeking greatness for himself. All had been born into slavery. All needed the same redemptive exodus from slavery. No one had hope for relief from their oppression until the Lord made it possible. While some exhibited arrogance and pride, one was by all accounts humble.

Biblical leadership rests at times upon unsuspecting and unlikely persons. The Apostle Paul wrote about God's profound way of selecting whom He will:

"But God has chosen the foolish things ... the weak things ... the base things ... the things which are despised ... and the things which are not, to bring to nothing the things that are, that no flesh should glory in His presence" (1 Corinthians 1:27-29).

Abraham ... Ruth ... Hannah ... David ... Amos ... the Twelve Apostles ... and among nations, Israel.

In Moses' deuteronomic review, he reminded Israel of its lowly status:

"The Lord did not set His love on you nor choose you because you were more in number than any other people; for you were the least of all people" (Deuteronomy 7:7).

Envious competition roused dissatisfaction with and rebellion against God's elected leaders. Aaron, Moses' older brother, second in command of all Israel, experienced this burden of leadership.

Aaron, a great grandson of Levi (third son of Jacob), was the object of envy by a distant relative, Korah (Exodus 6:16-25), who was also a descendant of Levi. Both were born into slavery. Both had need of the same redemptive exodus. Neither had hope of relief from their oppression until the Lord made it possible. One was by all accounts humble; the other, a want-to-be usurper.

Korah challenged the right of Aaron to his very exalted position over the people as high priest. Filled with envy, and probably sneering with the cynical belief that he would replace Aaron, he brought 250 tribal leaders and confronted Aaron and Moses. Members of this rebel faction most likely wanted to be priests, rather than servants of priests: "You take much upon yourselves, for all the congregation is holy, every one of them, and the Lord is among them. Why then do you exalt yourselves above the assembly of the Lord?" (Numbers 16:1). Did they not consider that neither Moses nor Aaron had chosen such exalted places for themselves?

"And no man takes this honor to himself, but he who is called by God, just as Aaron was" (Hebrews 5:4). Holy offices are never legitimately the choices of men. At this juncture all Israel would know upon whom God had laid His hand for this high honor: "That one whom He chooses He will cause to come near to Him ... the man whom the Lord chooses is the holy one" (Numbers 16:5b,7).

The terrifying measures taken by the Lord to substantiate Aaron's election came quickly: the earth swallowed up the leaders of the rebels, and holy fire consumed the rest (see Numbers 16:20-35). Not even that drama seemed convincing enough. Rather than accepting those momentous signs, their hearts beat with a new complaint: "You have killed the people of the Lord" (Numbers 16:41). Again the Lord demonstrated His displeasure, this time by a plague, stopped only by the mediation of Aaron himself: "And he stood between the dead and the living; so the plague was stopped" (Numbers 16:48).

Three testimonials certified Aaron's legitimacy. One more sealed it in their memory. The Lord commanded that each tribe bring a representative rod (staff, symbol of responsible authority) to Moses. Moses then laid them in the Holy of Holies before the Ark of the Testimony, Aaron's among them. Moses' rod had already shown its owner's power over nature in the presence of Pharoah; now Aaron's rod would settle his authority over God's people.

"Now it came to pass on the next day that Moses went into the tabernacle of witness, and behold, the rod of Aaron, of the house of Levi, had sprouted and put forth buds, had produced blossoms and yielded ripe almonds" (Numbers 17:8). Upon seeing this, the congregation fearfully accepted Aaron's divine ordination.

The rod itself produced buds like an almond tree branch, but the other tribal rods remained dead wood. "Almond" in Hebrew is *shaqed*, defined as that which "awakes." The same root word relates to "watchfulness." It is the first of the fruit trees to blossom at the beginning of the year. It awakens before others. So also, Aaron is the "first" regarding spiritual position and holy things. His election made him so, and he knew it, while his competitors only presumed it could come simply by human desire. It is not true that one may become anything one wants to be. That is a godless thought.

The blossoming rod compares to the Golden Lampstand inside the Tabernacle (Exodus 25:31-40). Each symbolized an instrument of "awakening" or illumination. The Lampstand gave light to the Holy Place; the Rod of Aaron certified him to be a source of illumination for all Israel. That required his personal vigilance and readiness to help Israel find its way.

A few times the prophets spoke of the anticipated Messiah as 'The Branch" (Jeremiah 23:5; 33:15; Zechariah 6:12). Jesus Himself said, "I am the true Vine ..." (John 15:1), and that He came as "... a light into the world ..." (John 12:46). John said, "That was the true Light which gives light to every man coming into the world" (John 1:9), and leads the way out of darkness.

The Tablets of Stone; the Bowl of Manna, prefiguring Jesus as the Life–giver; the Blossoming Rod of Aaron. What a wonder to think that these, in their material ways, housed as memorials in the Ark, clearly speak of our Incarnate Lord. These, along with all Tabernacle features, are like object lessons to those in spiritual kindergarten. Consider each carefully—they teach of the life and works of Jesus. They serve as sermons of grace, and draw us into greater devotion to Him, into closer accord with who He is and what He does.

The Tabernacle holds more forms that further reveal the character and purpose of God.

Aaron's Budding Rod

The objects in the Ark of the Covenant show God's mind toward us, and embody those qualities of the holy existence He created us to have as creatures made in His image. But these honors were sealed beneath a lid to show the price necessary to gain those gifts. The lid of the Covenant Ark was called the Mercy Seat, or the *Kapporet* (covering). It was the place where once a year the high priest acted out God's instructions for covering the sins of the nation through the sprinkling of blood on the Day of Atonement (Leviticus 16). On that day, when the smoke of the incense placed by the high priest in the Holy of Holies had covered the Mercy Seat, he came in twice with blood, first to atone for his own sins, and last for the sins of the nation.

The mercy seat was uniquely formed out of pure gold.

"And you shall make two cherubim of gold; of hammered work you shall make them at the two ends of the mercy seat ... of one piece with the mercy seat. And the cherubim shall stretch out their wings above, covering the mercy seat with their wings, and they shall face one another; the faces of the cherubim shall be toward the mercy seat" (Exodus 25:18-20).

"After [the Lord] drove the man out, He placed on the east side of the Garden of Eden cherubim and a flaming sword flashing back and forth to guard the way to the tree of life" (Genesis 3:22-24).

The lid was pure gold. Nothing indicates that it had a wooden interior, though some have thought so. Two cherubim of gold rose up out of the lid, hammered into shape and position as if rising up out of the lid itself. This was to become the place of the Presence of God. Its initial purpose was that of mediation.

## The Cherubim

Cherubim came into human history beginning with humankind's spiritual death in Eden's Garden:

> "So He drove out the man; and He placed cherubim at the east of the garden of Eden, and a flaming sword which turned every way, to guard the way to the tree of life" (Genesis 3:24).

Even after man had eaten from the tree of life, corrupting his nature with forbidden fruit, the possibility of restoration remained implicit. The cherubim stand on guard to direct the flow of events toward the day when access to the tree of life is re–opened.

> "To him who overcomes I will give to eat from the tree of life, which is in the midst of the Paradise of God" (Revelation 2:7).

Cherubim at Eden's gate stood as sentries. No one could pass. Cherubim are traditionally included in the angelic order, other members being seraphim, archangels, or simply angels (though there may be other categories also). Angels are described as "greater in power and might" (2 Peter 2:11) than humans, a fact demonstrated at times in Old Testament history (2 Samuel 24:16; Isaiah 37:36).

Ezekiel 1:4-26 depicts them in their role as part of the living chariot of God. John also saw them in a similar fashion in his visions in the Apocalypse (4:6-11). These references do not name them as "cherubim," and their designation as "living creatures" and no proof inidicates that they are cherubim in either Ezekiel or the Apocalypse. But David wrote about their closeness to God in a psalm: "And He rode upon a cherub, and flew; He flew upon the wings of the wind" (Psalm 18:10).

Not too much is disclosed in Scripture about their nature or form. But they hold great importance in the divine plan, and somehow have part in ministry to us, represented by their position upon the Mercy Seat.

When Solomon built the Temple, he placed the Ark of the Covenant and Mercy Seat in the Holy of Holies, and added two other figures. They were also cherubim, but of great stature (possibly 18 feet), made of olive wood. Their wings stretched across the Oracle from wall to wall, one wing of each cherub touching a wing of the other, the other wing of each extending to the wall on its side of the Oracle. They overshadowed the Ark of the Covenant and Mercy Seat (1 Kings 6:23-28).

Solomon's Temple was much larger and more complex than the original Tabernacle carried by the Israelites. Perhaps this is why these figures fill up the great open space of the Holy Cubicle. But the Lord Himself designed the Temple as well as the Tabernacle, having given the instructions to King David (1 Chronicles 28:19), and God makes nothing without purpose.

# Cherubim and Christ

Angels appear often in the life of Jesus, according to the following chronology:

At Jerusalem (Luke 1:11-20)
At Nazareth (Luke 1:38; Matthew 1:18-23)
At Bethlehem (Luke 2:8-15; Matthew 2:13, 19, 20)
In Judean wilderness (Luke 4:11)
In Gethsemane (Luke 22:43)

When Jesus agonized over his impending trial and execution in the garden of Gethsemane, the appearance of an angel may have special significance as it relates to the cherubim of the Oracle.

Jesus prayed under the trees in Gethsemane, where even today aged olive trees grow and produce their fruit. Some may date back to those agonizing moments experienced by the Lord Jesus just before His betrayal and arrest. In the course of His praying, an angel came to strengthen Him. Then He continued in even more strenuous prayer. Under the shadows of gnarled olive limbs and angel presence, Jesus prayed, sweat from His body falling to the ground like great drops of blood. It was the Lord of the Temple bringing His Oracle to a garden, the same environment where the first humans dwelled. This time the original purpose would be made right. By the shedding of blood, He initiates His sacrifice, and engages people along the way to participate in its completion. He is the Living Oracle, and all that is associated with a Temple points to Him, the fulfiller of Law, the sustainer of life, the personal brightness of the Father's light. He is the means of covenant. He is also the means of mercy.

## Mercy

At least three Greek terms used in the New Testament are translated as "mercy." (The noun form is given here, though the references also use the verb form of each.)

*Eleos*—the general term, connoting the thought or awareness of a need for mercy (Matthew 5:11).
*Splangchnon*—more specifically, compassion, the feeling of mercy as described of Jesus (Matthew 9:36).
*Hilasmos*—the act of mercy, especially in expiating the sinner, the "covering" petitioned by the Publican whose prayer revealed his need for the benefits of the Mercy Seat (Luke 18:9-14).

The last word, *hilasmos*, is akin to the word *hilasterion*, a form of which appears in the Septuagint translation from Hebrew to Greek in the Exodus passage about the Mercy Seat. The Apostle Paul applied the word *hilasterion* to Jesus in Romans 3:25: "God presented [Christ] as a sacrifice for atonement [*hilasterion*], through faith in His blood. He did this to demonstrate His justice, because in His forbearance He had left the sins [*hilasterion*] committed beforehand unpunished ..."

Jesus is the Living Mercy Seat, the means for covering sin, the Reconciler between God and man, through whose blood we have covenant privileges. He and He alone is the

Way to God, the Truth about God and the Life from God. If grace is effected, it is because of Him, truly God and truly Man.

> "For there is one God and one Mediator between God and men, the Man Christ Jesus, who gave Himself as a ransom for all men—the testimony given in its proper time" (1 Timothy 2:5,6).

## Cherubim and Eternity

The cherubim of the Mercy Seat might represent us—as we shall be in our glorified condition when fully redeemed. It may well illustrate our reverential pose before the Savior in that day when we see Him, the source of our salvation. We shall be like the angels, though we have what they cannot claim—the covering of His blood and the witness of His Spirit within our tabernacle of flesh.

"Make a lampstand of pure gold and hammer it out, base and shaft; its flowerlike cups, buds and blossoms shall be one piece with it" (Exodus 25:31).

Ministering priests assigned to various tasks within the Holy Place saw a room of great beauty as they passed through the veiled doorway. As with the golden walls of the Most Holy Place, the walls of this first sacred room gleamed mirrorlike, the source of its brightness coming from the Seven–branched Menorah. The Holy of Holies on the other side of the Separating Veil would have greater radiance only when the Shekinah Glory of God was manifested. In the oil light of the Lampstand the priests could see the other holy furniture, the Golden Altar of Incense, and the Golden Table of Showbread. Common priests beheld things that people not of the priestly tribe were forbidden to look upon. Even the Levites who carried the Tabernacle and furnishings from place to place throughout the wilderness sojourn could not look at the holy furniture. Before they moved the Tabernacle, every item was by specific instruction covered by the priests with cloths or animal skins (Numbers 4:1-33). Only those consecrated sons of the bloodline of Aaron were allowed to see these holy things.

## Form

The Lampstand was made of pure, solid gold. The dimensions are not given, but weight and design are. No wood formed its frame, but it was hammered into shape as a single piece. The middle shaft, base and branches were one—no seam appeared where one part extended from another, but was unified throughout—as if it had naturally grown that way. Branches depicted the development of the almond tree, each branch symmetrical with the others.

## Almond Tree

The almond tree symbolizes "watchfulness" or "readiness" (see Jeremiah 1:11,12) . Here is the "almond tree" of worship, the blossoming of light. This genus of trees, among the first to "awaken" out of winter sleep, signals that the light of Spring has come and calls forth fruit.

The branches of the Lampstand extended from each side of the central shaft and curved upward to the height of the other branches, three on the right side, three on the left. In the stem of each branch the craftsman formed something like leaves, buds, and flowers; and on the top of each branch a "lamp" or vessel for pure olive oil was set.

## Olive Oil

Each evening, a priest refilled the Holy Lamp. The Jewish day still begins in the evening and ends in the evening of the next day. Traditionally, only the light on the central shaft burned throughout the day, but at evening, the beginning of a new day, all branches were to burn. The custom brings to mind the Creation account—the light of each day of creation shines out from night's beginning hours. The olive oil would soak into the wick of each lamp and fuel seven flames of light that flickered throughout the darkness until the morning dawned. It would all be trimmed and re–kindled the following evening.

Shadow and Substance

"Command the children of Israel that they bring you pure oil of pressed olives for the light, to make the lamps burn continually. Aaron shall be in charge of it from evening until morning before the Lord continually" (Leviticus 24:1-4).

The way the oil for the bowl was prepared has spiritual significance, and parallels the passion of our Lord. Once plucked, the olive was crushed until its pure essence slowly drained from its torn flesh, then it was consecrated for holy use—some to be blended with spices for anointing (Exodus 30:22-33), some to burn in the Lampstand. It models Gethsemane, "the oil press," where Jesus already had begun to feel the weight of His crushing ordeal (Matthew 26:36-39; Luke 22:39-44). We have the Essence, because He was "crushed" for our iniquities, and the oil of His life illumines in us the things of God. Oil aflame is reduced by burning. The gold of His refined life stands flawless, holding forth the Oil of His revealing light.

"He is the True Light which gives light to every man coming into the world" (John 1:9).
"I am the light of the world. He who follows me shall not walk in darkness, but have the light of life" (John 8:12).
"As long as I am in the world, I am the light of the world" (John 9:5).
"The people who walked in darkness have seen a great light" (Isaiah 9:2).

## History
Young Samuel, apprentice to Eli, observed the dimming of many lights in Israel—the prophetic light was rare; the priestly light was blurred; the sanctuary light was going out. Not

much of a message was heard; not much of a ministry was served; not even much of a meaningful ritual remained to remind Israel of God.

Blessed Israel had its luminaries: Moses, Joshua, Samuel, David, Solomon, Hezekiah, Josiah, Elijah, Elishah, Isaiah, Jeremiah—but at last, the darkness overcame the nation through sin, and the citizens were forced into captivity by Babylon. Toward the end of that captivity, an infamous banquet was held in Babylon by Belshazzar, co–regent of the empire. While the guests sipped from Jerusalem's holy vessels, it may have been the Golden Lamp-stand itself that reflected its light upon a nearby wall.

"In the same hour the fingers of a man's hand appeared and wrote opposite the lamp-stand on the plaster of the wall of the king's palace ... MENE, MENE, TEKEL, UPHARSIN ... Belshazzar, your days have run out, you lack weight in the balances, your kingdom is split" (Daniel 5:25).

Beginning with the new Persian rule, the time of Israel's captivity time had also ended.

A small portion of the exiled Judeans returned to Jerusalem, carrying with them the sacred treasures to rebuild the Temple. Within 400 years the Lamp of God would survive the tyranny of Antiochus Epiphanes and regain strength through the Macabbean revolt. Enough consecrated oil was found amid the rubble of a defiled Temple to burn upon the Lamp for one day. Miraculously, it burned for eight days. "Hanukkah" or "The Feast of Dedication" is a celebration of the singular event (John 10:22,23).

## Prophetic Visions

Zechariah, a post-exilic prophet, had a vision of the Lampstand (Zechariah 4:1-14) that reveals what it really stood for.

> " ... there is a lampstand of solid gold with a bowl on top of it, and on the *stand* seven lamps with seven pipes to the seven lamps. Two olive trees are by it, one at the right of the bowl and the other at its left" (Zechariah 4:2,3).

> "These are the two anointed ones, who stand beside the Lord of the whole earth" (Zechariah 4:14).

The Gold Lampstand

It becomes clear through Zechariah's words that the Tabernacle Lampstand is but a shadow of Lord Jesus Christ. This is not just a fanciful interpretation, but truth confirmed in the Transfiguration of Jesus, where Moses and Elijah stood on either side of Him and conversed about His "exodus" (Luke 9:28-36). It seems probable that those two witnesses mentioned in Revelation 11:1-14 are the same men.

In his writings about the vision he had while on the island of Patmos, the Apostle John attests that he saw Jesus as never before, standing in the midst of seven golden lampstands (Revelation 1:13). The mysterious portrayal among the lampstands refers to Jesus' relation to the Church. Jesus is the Lightgiver, and He has ordained to shine through us the knowldge of God and His redeeming love. The Church should resemble Him.

## The Rod and the Lamp

The Lampstand with its gold and light symbolizes the divinity of Jesus; Aaron's Rod, with its earthly wood, symbolizes the humanity of Jesus. One projects an earthly branch in heavenly places; one a heavenly branch in earthly places. There would be no light for common men had not Jesus the Son of God shone into their humble existence to give them light on earth; there would be no reason to give light had not Jesus the Son of Man become the living Covenant who holds the rod of all authority in earth and heaven.

Shadow and Substance

#  The Table of Showbread

"Make a table of acacia wood ... Overlay it with pure gold and put a gold molding on the rim. ... Put the bread of the Presence on this table to be before Me at all times" (Exodus 25:23-30).

Etched into the table before the pulpit in many churches are the words "This Do in Remembrance of Me." Others have the words "Holiness Unto the Lord." The ancient Tabernacle also had a table to which both phrases apply. By the north wall of the Holy Place stood the Table of Showbread, about two feet high, three feet long, and one and one–half feet wide. A gold overlay completely covered its acacia wood frame. Every Sabbath day the priests removed the seven–day–old bread loaves and replaced them with new. The ceremony had become rather rigid by the time of Jesus. It was a sacred service to perform, and no doubt in the initial days of its observance, the priest responsible approached the exchange reverently, with sensitivity. Let us approach its meaning with the same attitude.

## Showbread and Manna

As discussed in chapter four, manna (the bread come down from heaven) foreshadowed Christ the Lifegiver in His divinity. The Showbread foreshadowed Him as the Lifegiver in His humanity, because of the process through which that bread was made acceptable for its holy purpose (see page 20). The intentions of both come together in Jesus, for He is mysteriously, but evidently, both God and Man, and from each of His natures God grants us life.

## From Grain to Bread

He is the Bread of heaven sent down from the Father; and He is the Bread of the Holy Place, the enjoyment of the priests. Under the old covenants, its nourishment was for an exclusive family; now, its fulfillment includes all the people of God. Before, the Showbread was wrought by the hands of men for placement in the Sanctuary: it was the "grain of wheat" sown, grown, scythed, winnowed, crushed, sifted, kneaded, formed, baked, and presented before the Lord on the golden table. Now it is the Incarnate Lord, virgin–born, perfectly grown, seasonably scythed, relentlessly winnowed, brutally crushed, submissively sifted, enigmatically enduring the kneading of judgment, fulfilling humiliation for our sins in the form of a slave through the fiery sentence of His Cross. He is the Perfect Bread, the One Bread, from whom, if we partake, our individuality is enhanced with His unity. It is because of His Incarnation and the process of His human life—from birth to burial to resurrection and ascension—that such a mingling is given.

> "I am the living bread which came down from heaven. If anyone eats of this bread, he will live forever; and the bread that I shall give is My flesh, which I shall give for the life of the world" (John 6:51).

## Leaven

Showbread must have no leaven, no yeast. Yeast is used in some Scripture to represent sin, particularly the sin nature with which we are born. Like bread affected by yeast, sin makes an exaggerated appearance, puffs up the self, boasts of more than it really has. Jesus warned His disciples of this falseness:

"'Beware of the leaven of the Pharisees and Sadducees' ... Then they understood that He did not tell them to beware of the leaven of bread, but of the
doctrine of the Pharisees and Sadducees"    (Matthew 16:6, 12)

"Beware of the leaven of the Pharisees, which is hypocrisy" (Luke 12:1).

One interpretation of the Parable of Leaven holds that the Church would, in the
course of its history, be influenced by the leaven of the world—the Church would become
like the world. That is a possible intent. It certainly has its examples. But that parable could
also have another meaning (or more): since Jesus used leaven to illustrate "the kingdom of
heaven," in this context He may be speaking of the kingdom's influence in the world. That
also has its manifold examples. But in the Exodus context, leaven apparently implies the sin
nature. No sin is allowed in the Holy Places.

## Christ's Bread

How beautifully our Lord comes into the world. He is sinlessly born in the town of
Bethlehem—the House of Bread. He is tempted of the devil to change a stone into bread at
the end of His forty days' fast in the wilderness. He miraculously feeds five thousand, then
four thousand, plus women and children, out of compassion for them. As they followed Him,
riveted upon His words and works, they were oblivious to all else. The multiplied sustenance
satisfied; and it illustrated the greater miracle of His power to feed all mankind spiritually
and for eternity. As He sat by the well in Samaria, Jesus told His disciples, "I have bread you
know not of" (John 4:32-34).

The Table of Showbread

## The Fellowship of Bread

The Apostle Matthew brings us to the Upper Room during that fateful Passover, briefly recording Jesus' act and words: "And as they were eating, Jesus took bread, blessed and broke it, and gave it to the disciples, and said, 'Take, eat; this is My body.'" He declared the wine His blood. The Apostle Paul acknowledged the Christian use of this Jewish supper, and related it also to the body of the Church. "For we, though many, are one bread and one body; for we all partake of that one bread" (1 Corinthians 10:17). Partaking of the same loaf individually makes us one corporately, for the same spiritual nourishment is in us all.

Two men met Jesus along the road to Emmaus from Jerusalem after leaving the holy city. They were discouraged after Jesus' execution and did not know who He was. But as they sat down in their humble Judean home, the Lord took bread as if He were the host of the table and broke it before them. Then their eyes were opened to His identity. It was not an arbitrary act, for He does nothing without a plan. He took the exclusive bread of the Temple to a new setting, an inclusive one, even for two alone in His presence. Here before them was the Table of His Life, and there before Him sat two priests of the new order.

One morning during the forty days after His resurrection, Jesus prepared breakfast for some who had decided, in spite of His amazing defiance of death, to go fishing. After all, there was no harm in fishing, and no rebuke was given to them. No fish were biting until Jesus spoke to them from the shore, "Children, have you any food?" They immediately recognized Him. His words must have brought back memories of other failed fishing ventures, and of His astounding intervention.

"Then, as soon as they had come to land, they saw a fire of coals there, and fish laid on it, and bread. Jesus then came and took the bread and gave it to them, and likewise the fish" (John 21:9,13).

His followers enjoyed such togetherness with Him in the Upper Room, the place of the Last Supper, and on the day He ascended into heaven and during their seven days' stay with Him. As they fed upon the Word of God and communed in prayer the Holy Spirit, like dew upon manna, fell upon them with purifying and enabling power. It soon became the practice to break bread from house to house, as the community of the Holy Spirit.

## The Bread and the Lamp

The Bread yet feeds the Body of Christ, but under the condition that we live in His grace, believe in His truth, and prove our love to Him and His people through obedience to His commands. The Table of Showbread and the Gold Lampstand should be found in every company of believers, just as they were designed for the Holy Place in the Tabernacle.

"But if we walk in the light as He is in the light, we have fellowship with one another, and the blood of Jesus Christ His Son cleanses us from all sin" (1 John 1:7).

## The Bread and the Frankincense

If we walk in the light of Christ's illuminating presence, we will share in the common Bread of His people. As we do, His blood has its cathartic, sin-cleansing effect among us. We may eat from His table if we have opened our hearts to His soul–searching light. There is no such sharing comparable to that for which believers have been prepared by being personally honest with God. Such wise honesty and true love carries over into our times together, formally and informally. A matrix of holy sweetness bonds the assembly of the saints—like frankincense upon unleavened loaves of bread, produced from the fields of personal labor, with the intent of festive presentation before the Lord.

Shadow and Substance

"Among those who approach Me I will show Myself holy; in the sight of all the people I will be honored" (Leviticus 10:1-3).

In front of the Tabernacle's inner veil, midway in the Holy Place, stood the Altar of Incense. Acacia wood framed its form, gold was its overlay. As with most of the furniture, the design had its specific dimensions (18 inches square by 36 inches tall), and its ornamentation (a gold molding around the top of the altar). It differed from the other pieces of furniture in one respect: projecting up from its four corners were "horns." By this it also correlated with the outside Altar of Bronze. The horns, like the horns of an animal, most likely represented the strength called for in completing the ministry. The horns of the Incense Altar were positioned to form a paradigm of penetrating prayer. The horns of the Sacrifice Altar outside were positioned as a paradigm of propitiating power.

"Let my prayer be as incense, the lifting up of my hands as the evening sacrifice" (Psalm 141:2).

## Meditation and Intercession

The Altar of Incense was not very tall, but its arrangement before the Veil leading into the Holy of Holies gave it special status. In fact, the New Testament nearly identifies it as belonging to the Most Holy Place.

"... and behind the second veil, the part of the tabernacle which is called the Holiest of All, which had the golden censer ..." (Hebrews 9:3,4).

This may be due to the flow of fragrant incense filling the air and filtering through the veil into the Oracle. It may also be due to its part in the Day of Atonement (Leviticus 16:12,13), when it was placed "inside the veil" to cloud the Mercy Seat.

It is a portrayal of our Great Intercessor, the Lord Jesus Christ, in His efficacious ministry of prayer, manifested in "unutterable groanings" (Romans 8:26)—while He was in the process of becoming our Mediator. This ministry led inevitably to the cross, and is manifested now, for "He ever lives to make intercession for us" (Hebrews 7:25).

## Incense

Components of the incense had two significant characteristics: the manner by which each was extracted, and the aroma each emitted.

"And the Lord said to Moses: 'Take sweet spices, stachte and onycha and galbanum, and pure frankincense with these sweet spices; there shall be equal amounts of each. You shall make of these an incense, a compound according to the art of the perfumer, salted, pure, and holy'" (Exodus 30:34, 35).

The special composition of incense they made was suited for burning on the altar. Each ingredient of the compound contributed its particular odor. The stachte is said to have been myrrh (Unger: "myrrh of tears"). Onycha has two possibilities: extracted either from a tree resin or from a mollusk shell. Galbanum was "a greasy, sticky, granulated resin, having a pungent odor and taste, which when mixed with fragrant substances, has the effect of increasing the odor and fixing it longer" (Unger). Frankincense likewise had a pungent odor, and seems, according to various Bible dictionaries, to be related to galbanum. Each spice was brought through a process of some kind to bring out its special character. Some were taken from a plant by incisions, some by roasting—all were pounded into a small dust–like consistency and blended "according to the art of the perfumer." Whether each had a symbolic intent or not, the whole compound so mirrored the essence of prayer—sweet submission, pungent petition, fiery passion, vaporous ascension, and propitiatory enabling.

## Ritual

The priests kept the incense burning perpetually, to show the ceaselessness of prayer. The incense was replenished just before daylight, and again at twilight, along with lighting or trimming the Gold Lampstand. It became a rare honor for a priest to burn the incense. King David divided the priests' duties into twenty–four courses, and each took his turn in carrying out the Tabernacle duties. Thousands of priests meant that each would serve for only a few days in sacred ministry. By the time of Zacharias (Luke 1:5-23), the chance of being the one to perform the ritual of burning the incense was minimal. Doctor Luke gives us the setting— Zacharias had been chosen by lot to attend the Altar of Incense, something he may never have done before, nor ever would have again. When Gabriel startled him there, he said, "Do not be afraid, Zacharias, for your prayer is heard ..." (Luke 1:13).

The ritual held that only a priest could minister before that small pulpit. But a Judean king named Uzziah (1 Chronicles 26:1-32) attempted to stand before that holy object. Uzziah (in 2 Kings 15 he is called "Azariah") found great favor with God and prospered exceedingly in his kingdom.

> "He sought God ... God made him prosper ... God helped him [in war] ... his fame spread ... he became exceedingly strong ... built towers ... fortified them ... dug many wells ... loved the soil ... had an army ... made devices in Jerusalem ... to shoot arrows and large stones ... But when he was strong his heart was lifted up, to his destruction, for he transgressed against the Lord his God by entering the temple of the Lord to burn incense on the altar of incense."

A king had no authority in the Holy Places of God's house, no right even to enter them. The priests reacted vehemently, commanding him to get out. There he stood defiantly, with censer of coals in hand, not immediately aware that leprosy suddenly appeared on his forehead. He had usurped the priests' authority, defiled the sanctuary, and brought shame to his position.

The Lord's appointments are certainties that cannot be trespassed without eventual consequence, not only for ancient Israel, but for the Church of Jesus Christ as well. It behooves us to know our parameters, and to honor that which God has established among us. Uzziah lost the honor of visible presence among his people—he was an excluded leper. We also can lose the same honor, and the leprosy of our sin will manifest its ugly, contagious, and excommunicative character.

Nonetheless, Uzziah was recognized as an effective king, and even a righteous man

(2 Kings 15:3). Isaiah remembers the year of his death, the year when he too had an experience before the Altar of Incense. (Some question whether he was in or outside of the Temple, but the vision indicates that he was inside.)

> "In the year that king Uzziah died, I saw the Lord sitting upon a throne, high and lifted up, and the train of His robe filled the temple... 'Woe is me, for I am undone! Because I a man of unclean lips, and I dwell in the midst of a people of unclean lips; for my eyes have seen the King, the Lord of hosts" (Isaiah 6:1,5).

As he stood in awe of this theophany, he responded as if he were leprous—"unclean lips." Could it have brought back memory of Uzziah's peril? Perhaps. He possibly thought, "I am as unclean as Uzziah; I am as unclean as any other man!" Then a seraph touched his mouth, declaring that his iniquity was taken away and his sin atoned for. The mention of such cleansing points to the coal. It had become an ember in the fire of the Bronze Altar.

It had participated in the bloodshed and burning of sacrifices. Upon the morning of that day its ministry had changed—a priest had carried it in a censer into the Holy Place, set it upon the Altar of Incense, and poured the powdered incense upon its small hot blaze. From the coal the melting incense vapored into the ambience of the Holy Place, the transforming catalyst sending it upward as if it were a fervent prayer. The meaning is evident. Prayer to the true and living God is made valid through the altar of sacrifice. Our access to the Father is based purely upon and dependent wholly upon the cross of our Lord Jesus Christ, the ultimate sacrifice. Isaiah's encounter with the seraph meant his cleansing from sin and his acceptance for service. Christian experience fulfills the ancient intention:

"Did not our hearts burn within us while He talked with us on the road, and while He opened the Scriptures to us?" (Luke 24:32)

"So God, who knows the heart, acknowledged them [Gentiles] by giving them the Holy Spirit, just as He did to us, and made no distinction between us and them, purifying their hearts by faith" (Acts 15:8,9)

## Acceptance

One other passage concerning the Altar of Incense pertains to the proper use of incense by the priests. It involves two priests who abused their positions.

"Nadab and Abihu, the sons of Aaron, each took his censer and put fire in it, put incense on it, and offered profane fire before the Lord, which He had not commanded them" (Leviticus 10:1)

The fire was profane, as opposed to holy fire, God's fire. Nahab and Abihu's source of ministry was not divine. Though they may have acted with good purpose, they acted out of order. Ministry has its appropriate behavior—the appropriated sanction and provision of God. These sons of Aaron were priests, ordained to holy positions. But they presumed that their status gave them liberty to do it their way.

The lesson remains for all time and eternity. God does not author confusion among His people. Rules of conduct have been set. The messages He gives through His servants place them under heavy obligation to speak by His Spirit, not by the pageantry of the flesh.

Nadab and Abihu received immediate judgment, lost their honor, perished by holy fire, and depleted the ministry of its needed servants. Their examples warn that the approach to God has been set by God, and has effect only by His own supply of power and direction.

## The Lawgiver

As the immutable laws of God speak of Jesus the Lawgiver, so does the Altar of Incense. The connection is found in their mutual purpose of reconciliation: the stone tablets set the rules for such a possibility; the incense sets the atmosphere for its actuation. It is the Law that must be fulfilled; it is the Spirit of Jesus who fulfills its moral requisites for us and in us. We know the Law and its mandates by conscience. We know the reckoning of our acceptance by the Lord's witness to our hearts that we are justified. By His work as Mediator the Law is engraved upon our hearts. He writes it there, and simultaneously sets the atmosphere for its keeping. The first ennobles us; the latter enables us for righteous and holy living.

Jesus is our Lawgiver, our Lifegiver, and our Lightgiver. These should include every faculty of our humanity, for through these things—law, life, and light—He has met the requirements for us who once were lawless, lifeless, and darkened. He met us in our utter depravity, placed Himself face to face with our dilemma, entered into our sin, imploded it with His glorious righteousness, restored us to the spiritual image we had lost, and freed us with His personal indwelling.

The Altar of Incense

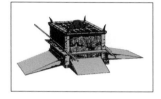

"Fire came out from the Presence of the Lord and consumed the burnt offering and the fat portions on the altar. And when all the people saw it, they shouted for joy and fell face–down" (Leviticus 9:22-24).

Patriarchal altars abounded, often named in accord with an incident in the patriarch's life. Genesis traces the use of altars from the beginning of human history. Though not specified, an altar is implied with Cain's and Able's offerings (Genesis 4:1-5). Noah knew to build an altar after the Flood (Genesis 8:20). In his journeys, Abraham marked nearly every place he walked through with an altar, the most notable being "Yahweh Yireh" at Mount Moriah (Genesis 22:13,14). Isaac (Genesis 26:25) and Jacob (Genesis 33:20; 35:7) built altars. The first Passover in Egypt required the doorposts and lintels of every home to become an altar (Exodus 12:1-14). Instructions for building a natural altar were given to Moses at the beginning of the Sinai experience (Exodus 20:22-26). Other altars were also made in later Israelite history, but here we focus upon the Bronze Altar that stood just beyond the entrance to the Tabernacle Court and in line to the east of the Tabernacle itself.

Acacia wood framed the Altar, bronze metal overlayed the frame. As with other Tabernacle furniture, the Levites carried the huge frame during the forty years' wilderness ordeal (Numbers 4:1-33). When Israel arrived at a new encampment, they filled the altar with dirt to raise its level to use for making sacrifices. The dirt was, of course, left behind when they moved onward to another place.

## Bronze

Bronze symbolizes judgment. The altar served as the place of vicarious judgment. There sin, the general name of an offense, could ritually receive pardon. The sinner was required to offer the prescribed sacrifice for the particular kind of sin committed (Leviticus 1:1-7:27).

Blood ran incessantly around the altar, for animal parts burned perpetually there. Blazing fire emitted waves of heat, and, as if replicating the Sun, brightened the surface of the Altar. It was a place of diligent work.

## Fire

After the craftsmen (Exodus 31:1-11) had finished their labors, a brief chronology of events followed from the Tabernacle dedication to the beginning of priestly ministry.

"And it came to pass in the first month of the second year, on the first day of the month, that the tabernacle was raised up ... And [the priest] put the altar of burnt offering before the door of the tabernacle of meeting, and offered upon it the burnt offering and the grain offering, as the Lord had commanded Moses ... Then the cloud covered the tabernacle of meeting, and the glory of the Lord filled the tabernacle" (Exodus 30:17,29,34).

A few days later, the Lord Himself sent fire upon the Altar.

"It came to pass on the eighth day that Moses called Aaron and his sons and the elders of Israel ...and Moses said to Aaron, 'Go to the altar, offer your sin offering and your burnt offering, and make atonement for yourself and for the people'... Then Aaron lifted his hand toward the people, blessed them, and came down from offering the sin offering, the burnt offering, and peace offerings ... Then the glory of the Lord appeared to all the people, and fire came out from before the Lord and consumed the burnt offering and the fat on the altar ...." (Leviticus 9:1,7,22-24).

"A fire shall always be burning on the altar; it shall never go out" (Leviticus 6:13). The intervening days between the first and the eighth of that month were those of priestly consecration (Exodus 29, especially verses 35-37). The altar had already been ablaze for seven days, ignited by human hands, but the Lord Himself gave approbation with His own fire on the eighth day. The obedient response of man was a "consecration"; the fiery work of God was a "sanctification."

## Mediation

The altar mediated between God and man in judgment, in salvation, in consecration, and in sanctification. There the extremes of guilt and innocence, offense and pardon, and law and grace met together.

"Mercy and truth have met together; righteousness and mercy have kissed" (Psalm 85:10). Could a better description of mediation be written? Its succinct phrases profoundly speak of an almost impossible point of reconciliation. No person or thing could bring such opposites together, unless we consider Jesus and His cross.

The bronze altar and its sacrifices, with all the associated gore and fury, typify Christ and Calvary. The day of His passion was the worst and best of days—the worst of deaths

The Bronze Altar

and the best of life; the greatest transcendence and the most intimate immanence—all brought together in the Person of Jesus Christ our Lord. The time, place, and ordeal of His crucifixion became the Bronze Altar.

### *Chalkolibanos*

Texts such as Psalm 22 and Isaiah 53 poignantly cry out with precise details those horrible moments Jesus endured for us, even as He knew throughout the joy that lay before Him. The Old Testament vividly presents the suffering of Jesus, but there are phrases in the New Testament that bring glimpses of it. An obscure verse relates to the Bronze Altar, found in an apocalyptic appearance of the Son of God:

> "I was in the Spirit on the Lord's Day, and I heard behind me a loud voice, as of a trumpet, saying, 'I am the Alpha and the Omega, the First and the Last'... Then I turned to see the voice that spoke with me ... One like the Son of Man ... His feet were like fine brass, as if refined in a furnace ...." (Revelation 1:10-12,15)

"His feet were like fine brass"—the key words being "fine brass." In the Greek text it is one word—*chalkolibanon*. As far as scholars are concerned, it is a rare word, occurring in the Bible only here and in Revelation 2:18. *Chalkolibanon* is a compound of two words, *chalkos* (the Greek word for brass/bronze), and *libanos* (the word for frankincense). "Brass frankincense" is an unlikely alloy, but not so strange when applied to Jesus, the One who has walked through the fiery bronze furnace of judgment for us, a sacrifice of sweet fragrance to God the Father.

It could also have a contrasting intent: our Lord has the right to judge all men—and He will; He also has the right to forgive—and He does. In accord with the austere symbol of brass, Jesus judges. In accord with the sweet symbol of frankincense, Jesus justifies—because "His feet were like fine brass, as if refined in a furnace ..."

## Altar to Altar

One other aspect of the Altar deserves notice: its connection with the Altar of Incense within the Holy Place, before the Veil. Both had "horns" projecting upward from the top at each corner. Horns speak of strength, both defensive and offensive. The horns of the Incense Altar typify the strength of Jesus' intercession; the horns of the Sacrifice Altar typify the strength of Jesus' vicarious endurance. A phrase from the Psalms alludes to this thought: "... Bind the sacrifice with cords to the horns of the altar" (Psalm 118:27).

The two altars had a ritual connection daily. From the Bronze Altar outside a priest took some embers, fiery coals used for consuming sacrifices, and then walked reverently toward the Altar of Incense inside the Sanctuary, placed them upon a receptacle on the Altar of Incense, and poured incense over the burning coals. The fragrance from the Altar of Incense was dependent upon the work first accomplished at the Altar of Sacrifice.

The last notion perhaps more directly applies to that strange word, *chalkolibanon*. In Christ the significance of the two altars are brought together. Jesus, our Heavenly High Priest, has passed through the fire of sacrifice on earth; and the burning remembrance of that experience was offered in the heavenly sanctuary as a sweet fragrance to God the Father (Ephesians 5:2; 2 Corinthians 2:14).

The Bronze Altar

The ancient Altar of Israel, awesome as it was in form and ritual, is as dust in the wind compared to the eternal work of our Lord.

"... we have such a high priest, who is seated at the right hand of the Majesty in the heavens, a minister of the sanctuary and of the true tabernacle ..." (Hebrews 8:1,2)

"We have an altar from which those who serve the tabernacle have no right to eat" (Hebrews 13:10).

Shadow and Substance

"Make a bronze basin, with its bronze stand, for washing. ... when they approach the altar to minister by presenting an offering made to the Lord by fire, they shall wash their hands and feet so that they will not die" (Exodus 30:17-21).

"He made the laver of bronze and its base of bronze, from the bronze mirrors of the serving women who assembled at the door of the tabernacle of meeting." (Exodus 38:8)

Gold, according to some sources, symbolizes Divinity. Silver symbolizes redemption. Bronze symbolizes judgment. The Laver and the Altar of Sacrifice were both made of bronze—the Altar with bronze overlay on an acacia wood frame, the Laver purely of bronze.

## Liturgical Basin

The Laver was a large basin serving as a place for priestly washing: "Aaron and his sons shall wash their hands and their feet from it" (Exodus 30:19). On the day of their consecration, the men in the family of Aaron were bathed completely (Exodus 29:4) before dressing in their liturgical garments. Then their ordination ceremony continued with certain sacrifices, blood, oil, and more sacrifices, by which to engage them fully in ministry.

Outside in the Court an array of sacrificial ordinances set the pattern of the work to be performed on the Altar, a bloody, sweaty labor. Inside the Tabernacle, the priests yielded acts of worship to God, a more delicate and sensitive work. The Laver stood between two places: the Court with its Bronze Altar, and the Holy Place with its Lampstand, Showbread

Table, and Incense Altar. The priests stopped to wash their hands and feet as they passed from one place to the other.

> "When they go into the tabernacle of meeting, or when they come near the altar to minister, to burn an offering made by fire to the Lord, they shall wash with water, lest they die. So they shall wash their hands and their feet, lest they die ..." (Exodus 30:20,21).

In other words, the priest must be clean as he ministers before God in the House of Worship; and he must be clean as he works at the altar with souls seeking peace with God. The preparation for either place was the Laver. Should one bypass the washings, he would die. All priests, Jewish and Christian, need the washing.

## A Mirror

Bazelel's craftsmen made the Laver "from the bronze mirrors of the serving women ..." (Exodus 38:8). Its size, shape, and decor are not given in the biblical description, but its use and symbolism are clear. We understand its refreshing function for Israel's priests. As priests approached the Laver, their image was reflected, perhaps revealing even the dirt upon their hands and feet.

The Bible is our Laver, as the Apostle James relates:

> "But be doers of the word, and not hearers only, deceiving yourselves. For if anyone is

a hearer of the word and not a doer, he is like a man observing his natural face in a mirror; for he observes himself, goes away, and immediately forgets what kind of man he was. But he who looks into the perfect law of liberty and continues in it, and is not a forgetful hearer but a doer of the work, this one will be blessed in what he does" (James 1:22-25).

The Word of God, when read, mirrors to us what we are.

## A Baptismal Font

The ritual of washing found new meaning in the baptismal work of John the Baptist, especially when he reluctantly baptized Jesus in the Jordan River. John was of priestly lineage. His parents Zachariah and Elizabeth were both descendants of Aaron. John had every right to enter the Temple Courts. Instead, God set him apart as a priest with another direction of priestly work: to announce the coming of Messiah. The Messiah was to emerge from the lineage of Judah, not the priestly family of Levi, and therefore had no natural rights to earthly priesthood (Hebrews 7:13,14). But He did come to be the true and heavenly high priest (Hebrews 7:25-8:2). If John's baptism reflects the Temple Laver, then at the Jordan we have one priest washing Another for ministry. Our Lord did priestly ministry after His baptism and anointing, for the full range of His work may be divided according to priestly responsibilities of teaching, preaching and healing (Matthew 4:23).

Immersion in the River Jordan under John the Baptist's hand also presents Jesus as "the Lamb of God who takes away the sin of the world" (John 1:29)—a sacrifice that also required washing before burning (Leviticus 1:10-13). It could be said that those who "follow

Jesus in baptism" must be aware of the cost of following Jesus "after baptism"—service and sacrifice!

## Upper Room Drama

In a dramatic Upper Room moment, Jesus furthered His priestly role. During the Passover ceremony, He rose from His host position, laid aside His garments and, humbling Himself before each apostle, washed their feet. It was a servant act, portraying His willingness to join us. It was a lordly act, in accord with His duty as the host. It was an act of salvation, foretelling His redemptive ordeal at Calvary. It was a high priestly act, pointing back to the Day of Atonement once a year in the Holy of Holies, and forward to His own eternally accepted atonement in the heavenly Holy of Holies.

## The Loutron

The meaning of the Laver continues to unfold in the writings of the Apostle Paul.

> "According to His mercy He saved us, through the washing of regeneration and renewing of the Holy Spirit ..." (Titus 3:5).

The Bible explains our salvation as a "washing (laver/loutron) of regeneration (new birth)." The New Testament word for "washing" is the same word used in Exodus 30:18 for "laver." This aligns beautifully with the Apostle John's statement about the death of Jesus: "But one of the soldiers pierced His side with a spear, and immediately blood and water came out" (John 19:34). That account brings altar and Laver together: blood from the Altar's lambs; water from the Laver's washings. Those elements issuing from Jesus' pierced side at His crucifixion are elements of birth, a thought which explains the Calvary scene and Paul's application of it.

## Holiness

One other passage has roots in the significance of the Laver. It refers not to initial salvation, but to the ongoing work of Jesus Christ in His people and parallels the constancy of priestly washings.

> "Husbands, love your wives, just as Christ also loves the church and gave Himself for her, that He might sanctify and cleanse her with the washing of the water by the word, that He might present her to Himself a glorious church, not having spot or wrinkle or any such thing, but that she should be holy and without blemish" (Ephesians 5:25-27).

The Greek phrase reads, "that He might sanctify, having cleansed her ..." The word for "cleanse" is *katharizo*—a catharsis from sin. Having washed her at the Laver of the Word, the Church [His Bride] might be made completely holy. The figure of the Laver and its water remind us of the intent of Jesus to cleanse us through hearing and responding to His Word. Through preaching and teaching under the authority of Scripture, we receive fresh cleansing. The Savior at the Altar must become the Sanctifier in His Word. And His voice [is] as the sound of many waters ..." (Revelation 1:15).

# The Linen Walls and the Veils

Linen cloth held up by bronze posts and silver hooks bounded the perimeter of the Tabernacle Court, the area pertinent to the daily priestly work. The bronze posts stood upright upon bronze sockets, anchored into the ground by pegs and by cords stretched to either side of the wall. Though a simple structure, its materials were of great value, its significance rich in typology.

Linen, as verified by use in the New Testament, signifies "righteousness."

"Hang the curtain from the clasps and place the ark of Testimony behind the curtain. The curtain will separate the Holy Place from the Most Holy Place" (Exodus 26:31-37).

"And to her [the Church] was granted to be arrayed in fine linen, clean and bright, for the fine linen is the righteous acts of the saints" (Revelation 19:8).

Silver has been used as a medium of exchange, and as a symbol of redemptive cost.

"... you were not redeemed with corruptible things, like silver or gold from your aimless conduct received by tradition from your fathers ..." (1 Peter 1:18).

Bronze is associated with judgment.

"And your heavens which are over your head shall be bronze ..." (Deuteronomy 28:23).

The linen walls forbade any to enter except through the front doorway, symbolizing the standard by which holiness would be given. Holiness blessings presuppose a state of righteousness. The two main conditions of Christian existence in this world are related to each other. Paul touches upon this briefly in Romans 6:19. "... so now present your members as slaves of righteousness for holiness."

The Holy Rooms were separated by a cherubic–embroidered veil, stretched across from side wall to side wall, like the diaphragm of a body. Its blue, purple, and scarlet threads were intricately blended with linen and hung between the Holy Places on four gold–leaf covered acacia pillars. It warned of an unapproachable holiness. Common priests could enter the main sanctuary through the first veil after having been made ceremonially clean. But only the high priest could pass beyond the second veil separating the Holy of Holies where sat the Ark of the Covenant. This veil taught how close man was (or was not) to God. Though ornate, it was there for more than cosmetic effect. Its placement signaled the ultimate point at which life and death met each other.

> "And the Lord said to Moses, 'Tell your brother not to come at just any time into the Holy Place inside the veil, before the Mercy Seat which is on the Ark, lest he die; for I will appear in the cloud above the Mercy Seat" (Leviticus 16:2).

> "into the second part [the Most Holy Place] the high priest went alone once a year ..." (Hebrews 9:7).

The whole passage not only tells of the high priest's limited access (Leviticus 16), but also the means by which he must pass through into the presence of God. Once a year, on the Day of Atonement (Yom Kippur), he was to cloud the forbidden room with incense, then sprinkle blood upon the Mercy Seat, first to atone for his own and his family's sins, then to atone for the whole nation.

The principal New Testament verses explaining this ritual are Hebrews 9:1-10:25. Verse 9:8 summarizes the divine purpose for the veil:

> "... the Holy Spirit indicating this, that the way into the Holiest of All was not yet made manifest while the first tabernacle was still standing."

God the Holy Spirit was involved in that ancient structure, from its material to its usage. Fickle as His people became, He Himself did not abandon the divine plan to reconcile us to God. Even captivity, dispersion, destruction, defilement, and subjection to foreign occupations had no power to annul the Tabernacle schema. Returning from Babylon, the chastened people anticipated rebuilding the House of God. This they accomplished, but not without opposition and hesitation (see Ezra and Nehemiah).

The rebuilt Temple was aesthetically inferior to Solomon's magnificent Temple. Herod the Great later enhanced its size and beauty, but its basic form followed "the pattern shown in the Mount." Each had two holy rooms divided by a veil. Tragedy came to each structure in the time of Nebuchadnezzar in 586 B.C., Antiochus Epiphanes in 166 B.C., and Titus in 70 A.D. But the prophets envisioned another sanctuary "in the latter days," when Messiah reigns over all things from Jerusalem (Isaiah 2:1-3).

## Correlation of the Veils

The Veils have great significance concerning Jesus. Their purpose was exclusion because of the wrath of God against sin. The Veils covering the passage into the sanctuary were multicolored, each color representative of something about the Savior.

Blue—His heavenliness/holiness
Purple—His royalty/majesty
Scarlet—His sacrifice/suffering
White linen—His purity/righteousness

These speak of Him, and of the blessings and character of the Christian life. Whoever passed through the Veil into that holy arena passed through something not of his own making, just as is our experience in Christ Jesus.

Upon entrance, the sinner encountered immediately the place of sacrifice, a means of salvation within the confines of righteousness. When God initiates our salvation, we experience His prevenient grace, by which the realization comes that we need an atoning sacrifice. Passing through the entrance signified inclusion because of the love of God toward the sinner. Then they could enjoy the intimacy of light, life, and law portrayed in the Holy Place. The veils bring us to our Lord's cross. There, in a deeply poignant scene, the Savior yielded up His spirit, having finished His redemptive work. In that moment the old exclusion ended and the new inclusion began. Note the Scripture's account:

"And Jesus cried out again with a loud voice, and yielded up His spirit. Then behold, the veil of the Temple was torn in two from top to bottom" (Matthew 27:50,51).

Shadow and Substance

"When they came to Jesus and saw that He was already dead, they did not break His legs. But one of the soldiers pierced His side with a spear, and immediately blood and water came out" (John 19:33,34).

"Therefore, brethren, having boldness to enter the Holiest by the blood of Jesus ... through the veil, that is, His flesh, and having a high priest over the house of God, let us draw near with a pure heart in full assurance of faith, having our hearts sprinkled from an evil conscience and our bodies washed with pure water" (Hebrews 10:19,20).

The spear physically pierced the outer veil of His body and penetrated the inner veil of His heart. From the reservoir of His heart issued forth elements of His love.

Jesus Christ is the Veil, the righteous passage through which we enter to access all the blessings of His fellowship. Indeed, the Father and the Holy Spirit have made us "accepted in the Beloved" Son. The Veil has never been thrown away in a spiritual sense, but abides, torn. If we dare pass through, we may know Him in the intimacy of His own being.

He envelopes us by His righteous Presence, awakens us to our drastic condition, and gives us a sense of our condemnation as we consider Christ's horrible payment for our sins. It but remains for us to respond in faith and repentance, or to reject Him and know the wrath of God against those who turn away from this most precious Gift of His Only Begotten Son. But having entered that Veil, having proceeded toward His Gift, we have right of passage through the other Veils leading further and further into our new status before

God. But, it is ever to be remembered that all our blessings, our full inheritance with Jesus, are because of His righteousness.

# Inside the Tabernacle

Left: The Lampstand was made of pure, solid gold. Hammered into shape as a single piece, the branches, the middle shaft, and base each extended from one another seamlessly, with a unity throughout—as if it naturally grew that way. The symmetrical branches depicted the development of the almond tree.

Right: The Table of Showbread. The Bread (Jesus) feeds the Body of Christ (the Church), but under the condition that we live in His grace, believe in His truth, and prove our love to Him and His people by obeying His commands. The Table of Showbread and the Gold Lampstand should be found in every company of believers.

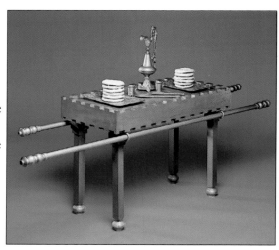

Right: The Bronze Altar, as it might have appeared in the Tabernacle courtyard. The altar served as the place of vicarious judgment. Here prescribed sacrifices for particular kinds of sin were offered (Leviticus 1:1-7:27).

The altar mediated between God and man. Blood ran incessantly around the altar, for animal parts burned perpetually there. The blazing fire brightened the surface of the Altar, signifying how God desires guilt and innocence, offense and pardon, and law and grace be reconciled through His presence. The Altar was an early revelation of God the Mediator, bringing salvation, consecration, and sanctification into the world.

In the center of the Holy of Holies stood the golden Ark of the Covenant. Three objects lay within it, each one representing something of God's nature and work: the stone tablets containing the Ten Commandments, Aaron's budding rod, and the manna. The Ark itself foreshadowed the actual presence of Christ, the Immanuel of Isaiah 7:14. Items in the Ark embodied qualities of Jesus' personhood as the Messiah, Yeshua, in relation to the world He came to save from sin (Isaiah 49:6,8 NKJV).

The material of the Ark itself conveyed the idea of God incarnate—pure gold for His divine nature, strong acacia wood for His durable manhood.

The Ark of the Covenant presents a portrait of the ultimate meeting place between God and humanity for reconciliation. It speaks of what is found in Christ once restoration has taken place: righteousness, life, victory over death, and the discovery of one's divinely appointed task.

"Now it came to pass on the next day that Moses went into the tabernacle of witness, and behold, the rod of Aaron, of the house of Levi, had sprouted and put forth buds, had produced blossoms and yielded ripe almonds" (Numbers 17:8). Upon seeing this, the congregation fearfully accepted Aaron's divine ordination.

The rod itself produced buds like an almond tree branch, but the other tribal rods remained dead wood. "Almond" in Hebrew is *shaqed*, defined as "that which awakes." The same root word relates to "watchfulness." It is the first of the fruit trees to blossom at the beginning of the year. It awakens before others. So also, Aaron is the "first" regarding spiritual position and holy things. His election made him so, and he knew it, while his competitors only presumed it could come simply by human desire.

The blossoming rod compares to the Golden Lampstand inside the Tabernacle (Exodus 25:31-40). Each symbolized an instrument of "awakening" or illumination. The Lampstand gave light to the Holy Place; the Rod of Aaron certified him to be a source of illumination for all Israel. That required his personal vigilance and readiness to help Israel find its way.

Left and Below: Outside in the Court an array of sacrificial ordinances led the pattern of salvific work upon the Altar, a bloody, sweaty labor. Inside the Tabernacle, the priests yielded acts of worship to God, a more delicate and sensitive work. The Laver stood between those two places, at which the priests must stop to wash their hands and feet as they passed from one place to the other.

"When they go into the tabernacle of meeting, or when they come near the altar to minister, to burn an offering made by fire to the Lord, they shall wash with water, lest they die. So they shall wash their hands and their feet, lest they die ..." (Exodus 30:20,21). In other words, the priest must be clean as he ministers before God in the house of worship; and he must be clean as he works at the altar with souls seeking peace with God. The Laver was the preparation place for both cleanings.

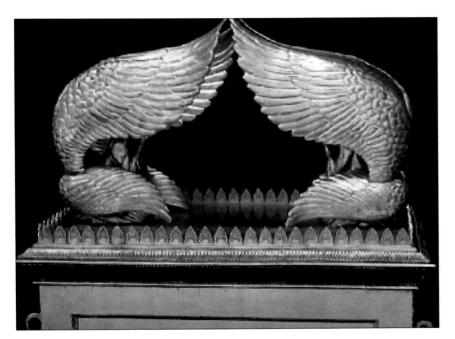

The lid of the Covenant Ark was called the Mercy Seat, or the *Kapporet* (covering). It was the place where once a year the high priest acted out God's instructions for covering the sins of the nation through the sprinkling of blood on the Day of Atonement (Leviticus 16). The mercy seat was uniquely formed out of pure gold. Nothing indicates that it had a wooden interior, though some have thought so. Two cherubim of gold rose up out of the lid, hammered into shape and position as if rising up out of the lid itself. This was to become the place of the Presence of God. Its initial purpose was that of mediation.

Cherubim at Eden's gate stood as sentries. No one could pass. Cherubim are traditionally included in the angelic order, other members being seraphim, archangels, or simply angels (though there may be other categories also). They hold great importance in the divine plan, and somehow have part in ministry to us, represented by their position upon the Mercy Seat.

effect. Its placement signaled the ultimate point at which life and death met each other.

Jesus Christ is the Veil, the passage through which we access all the blessings of His fellowship. Indeed, the Father and the Holy Spirit have made us "accepted in the Beloved" Son. The Veil has never been thrown away in a spiritual sense, but abides, torn. If we dare pass through, we may know Him in the intimacy of His own being.

Linen cloth held up by bronze posts and silver hooks bounded the perimeter of the Tabernacle Court. The bronze posts stood upright upon bronze sockets, anchored into the ground by pegs and by cords stretched to either side of the wall. Though a simple structure, its materials were of great value, its significance rich in typology.

The Holy Rooms were separated by a cherubic–embroidered veil, stretched across from side wall to side wall, like the diaphragm of a body. Its blue, purple, and scarlet threads were intricately blended with linen and hung between the Holy Places on four gold–leaf covered acacia pillars. It warned of an unapproachable holiness. Common priests could enter the main sanctuary through the first veil after having been made ceremonially clean. But only the high priest could pass beyond the second veil separating the Holy of Holies where sat the Ark of the Covenant. This veil taught how close man was (or was not) to God. Though ornate, it was there for more than cosmetic

# The Substance of the Tabernacle

"And walk in love, as Christ also has loved us and given Himself for us, an offering and a sacrifice to God for a sweet smelling aroma" (Ephesians 5:2).

"The One named Blessed, who is the God and Father of our Lord Jesus Christ, the One who blessed us with all spiritual blessings in the heavenlies, in Christ, inasmuch as it was in Him, that is, in Christ, He decided in our favor, before the universe was founded, that we must be holy, this decision constituting the plan for those of us who believe, to live in the spiritual blessing of purity, and without fault, living in the spiritual blessing of wholeness before God and men ..." (see Ephesians 1:3).

The writings of the Apostle Paul awaken our minds to living ecosystems of theological thought. His sentences form lengthy catenas of interdependent propositions, perfectly in accord with each other. Exclude one phrase or word and it is like a meadow filled with varied species and habitats, imbalanced by even the slightest human interference.

The Apostle Peter called Paul's epistles "... hard to understand, which untaught and unstable people twist to their own destruction, as they do also the rest of the Scriptures" (2 Peter 3:16). As with all of the inspired authors of the Bible, the thoughts presented often seem hard to follow, difficult to read in a breeze. Pauline letters have tremendously concentrated statements, and each is a well of truth. However, the explorer will find them all reaching down to the same body of water.

Another difficulty with Paul's correspondence regards finding the context. I can only lift words from a passage, and accurately teach them, when I fully understand the ground in which they were planted. I dare not fail to see how Paul's theological ecosystem holds together.

One powerful note of communication with Paul resonates in his tendency to repeat references to the Lord Jesus Christ. The Ephesian epistle breathes the name of Christ into every point, especially in the phrase, "in Christ." Everything "in Christ" affects what happens "in us" who believe.

Shadow and Substance

> Jesus says it is like the grape vine and its fruitful branches (John 15:1-8).Paul says it is like the olive tree with its natural and grafted branches  (Romans 11:16a-25).

> Jesus says it is like bread from heaven (John 6:48-58). Paul says it is like eating from the same loaf of bread (1 Corinthians 10:16,17).

> Jesus says it is like bearing a cross (Matthew 16:24). Paul says it is like being crucified with Christ (Galalians 2:20; 6:14).

Those "spiritual blessings" of Ephesians 1:3 appear in word after word, sentence after sentence, abounding even in the first chapter, showing Paul to have had the foresight of a prophet, the insight of a psychologist, the hindsight of a philosopher, and the oversight of a pastor. Articulation of those words causes thoughts to rise upon the horizon of our minds that would never dawn upon us otherwise. Careful concentration upon this and any part of

God's Word opens the spiritual eyes to spiritual dimensions sometimes beyond the grasp of explanation.

To be sure that we are not writing "eisegetically," reading into a truth our private opinion, be assured that the Ephesian letter does allude to the construction of the "Tabernacle" (and Temple) by Jesus, the Risen One:

"... from whom the whole body, joined and knit together by what every joint supplies, according to the effective working by which every part does its share, causes growth of the body for the edifying of itself in love" (Ephesians 4:16).

"... in whom the whole building, being fitted together, grows into a holy temple in the Lord, in whom you also are being built together for a dwelling place of God in the Spirit" (Ephesians 2:21,22).

"For He Himself is our peace, who has made both (Jew and Gentile) one, and has broken down the middle wall of separation" (Ephesians 2:14).

"And walk in love, as Christ also has loved us and given Himself for us, an offering and a sacrifice to God for a sweet smelling aroma" (Ephesians 5:2).

These are precious mysteries, designed for us before the foundation of the world. Jesus said, "It has been given to you to know the mysteries of the kingdom of heaven" (Matthew 13:12).

Returning to the idea of having "every spiritual blessing in the heavenly places, in Christ," let us raise the question, "What are they?" I suggest two categories of spiritual blessings in this sanctuary storehouse of our Lord:

1. His Character as produced in the Fruit of the Spirit, i.e., His love–nature
2. His Charisma as presented in the Favors of the Spirit, i.e., His power–gifts

In a way these two categories overlap. Jesus Christ does what He is, and what He is permeates all He does. His labor exudes from His life.

Shadow and Substance

# Christ's Character and Charisma

Like the robe of the ephod's ornamented pomegranates, the spiritual fruit is rich in beauty, and necessary for communion between the Lord and His people.

A great white cloud provided the canopy for the high priest's commissioning venue, tempering mountain breezes as they swept across the encampment of the Israelites on the wide plateau below the Sinai. There, below the Sinai corps, stood a man dressed in blue, other vestments also draping military–style from his stately frame. It was the occasion of his ordination. His full uniform, newly tailored, in tones of blue, purple and scarlet thread embroidery upon tightly woven linen cloth and intertwined with strands of gold, heightened the sacred moment. The blue robe formed a soft background to the other clothing worn over it.

The Lord called the blue clothing "the robe of the ephod" (Exodus 28:31-35). It did not have seamed sides, though "a woven binding" formed the opening for Aaron's head to slip through. From the skirted hem of the robe hung braided pomegranates of blue, purple, and scarlet thread, the colors of some of Aaron's upper vestments. The fine shapes were interspersed with small golden bells. When the high priest Aaron entered the "Holy Places," the bell would be heard, somewhat muffled by the fruit–forms between them. He dare not come before the Lord unannounced.

Writers have given a number of interpretations to this priestly attire, based on Scripture. With the New Testament imparting the knowledge that Jesus Christ is our Great High Priest, a better understanding of that role derives from Aaron's duties and garments.

Displaying "glory and beauty" (Exodus 28:2) as He walked among the common priests, he in many ways symbolized the Person and work of Jesus, even down to the fruit and bells of the robe's hem. The pomegranates symbolize our Lord's "Fruit of the Spirit," the bells His "Gifts of the Spirit."

When our Lord was crucified, soldiers divided His clothing among themselves (there were four separate pieces), and gambled over His long seamless tunic (John 19:23,24). Scripture wastes no words, so we may accept the account as having significance.

His seamless robe had no fruit and bells hanging from its lower part, but it did have a "hem." (If not upon that part of His clothing, probably from His mantle.) The Greek term for that hem is *kraspedon*, referring to the intricately tied strands hanging from the four corners of the Jewish prayer cloth. The hem, or *kraspedon*, would have been touched by the multitudes who reached out for healing as He passed by. They

> "... begged Him that they might only touch the hem of His garment. And as many as touched it were made perfectly well" (Matthew 14:36).

His healing power yet avails for any sickness—physical, emotional, intellectual, social—and necessarily for the infirmities of spiritual sin. When such healing comes, we trace it not only to the mercy of God, but to the nature of Jesus—His habit, yes, but moreover, His very character. That provision is like sap running from a vine into its branches. Such is the work of God the Holy Spirit, who brings to us the things of Jesus (John 16:14), replicating in the Christian heart the essence of the true Vine.

The Apostle Paul calls this "the Fruit of the Spirit" (Galatians 5:22,23). Like the. robe of the ephod's ornamented pomegranates, the spiritual fruit is rich in beauty, and necessary for communion between the Lord and His people.

The Fruit of the Spirit hang in three clusters of three each. Since they teach of the character of Jesus, they first exemplify His manner of relationship, then ours. The first three—love, joy, peace—reveal His respect toward God; the second cluster—longsuffering, gentleness, goodness—His respect toward others; and the third cluster—faithfulness, meekness, self–control—His self–respect. As we contemplate Jesus' character in these clusters, let us see if these supernatural savors appear in us, in what season of growth they are in, and if any have ripened sufficiently to refresh others.

This sort of fruit is inimitable, nor can it be hybrid. Its flavor and fullness  are obviously different, obviously "richer, deeper, sweeter." Without Jesus, human endeavors to grow a personality like His result in spoiled, rancid, stale, bitter fruit. When it is from God, it is as different as wine is from water used for ritual hand–washing. Let us taste and see how good is the Lord.

Christ's Character
and Charisma

# Christ's Character in the Fruit of the Spirit

"But the fruit of the Spirit is love, joy, peace, longsuffering, gentleness, goodness, faithfulness, meekness, self-control" (Galatians 5:22,23).

## Love (agape)

We know the definitions of God's love, but do we know its character and its work?

Jesus' love is divine. "God is love," says John (1 John 4:8). That is more than an attribute, as if it were some part of His attitude. It is the source of His demeanor and pervades all He is and all He does.

"In Christ," the greatest of "spiritual blessings in the heavenlies" is love. Take everything you know about God's nature, and love is there. His "ad intra," the intersphering of the members of the Trinity among Themselves, "moves" with love. His "ad extra," the whole of Creation, was made in love. His omniscience—His all-knowing—is in love. His omnipresence—His everywhere immanence—is in love. His omnipotence—His all-powerful ability—is in love. He preserves all things by the all-pervading care of love. He governs and judges every morally responsible creature by the determinations of love.

We know the definitions of God's love, but do we know its character and its work? Scripture, given as a call from love, is inspired by love, and its interpretation must have love as its guide. Otherwise, the tabernacle of our fellowship is but an empty house.

Certainly, this divine love is self–giving, and abundant. Christ at Calvary poignantly demonstrated that. But Calvary, the sacrifice of God's Only Begotten Son, not only signals reconciliation between God and man, it also stands for propitiation, and propitiation involves judgment to make that reconciliation possible. Jesus' crucifixion is a love act which commands and enables righteousness, and nurtures holiness in the souls of His followers.

Love is like Solomon's Temple pillars—strong, tall, guardians to the entrance of the Sanctuary. He named one pillar "Jachin" and the other pillar "Boaz." Jachin translates "He will establish"; Boaz translates "in it is strength" (1 Kings 15-22). Pomegranates, lilies, and chain wreaths were part of their ornamentation, and they were made from brass. "Boaz" also chronicles a love story through that divinely guided messianic line leading to Jesus. "Jachin" may represent the prophetic promise of divine assurance that Israel will not cease to be. Neither will love, as correctly understood. Love is strong. Its heights reach beyond the heavens, its beauty exceeds the lilies, its fruit abounds more than delectable pomegranates, and it guards its possessions with firmly placed pillars of judgment.

How grateful we are that the Bible balances its own propositions. By it we know what love is, and by it we know what love is not. While we enjoy the fruit, care also must be given to guard against the diseases which spoil it, or the inferior stock which seeks to replicate it. For that we have the guidance of 1 Corinthians 13, and an added personal supposition for contrast.

### Love's Homily

Love is neither brash nor brassy, not merely gifted nor merely giving.
Love suffers wrong, without losing its composure.

Love is kind, without losing its perception.

Love fervently desires, without rivalry.

Love is not ostentatious, though its credibility easily manifests itself. Love is not obnoxious, but gently forms its aura.

Love seeks no mere personal gratification, neither loses self–identity. Love is not irritable, neither loses its pungence.

Love harbors no bitterness against evildoers, neither dulls its memory.

Love has no pleasure in revenge, neither overlooks righteous standards.

Love has pleasure in truth, without ignoring grace.

Love conceals all things, without loss of trust.

Love believes all things, without loss of integrity.

Love hopes all things, without loss of reason.

Love endures all things, but not without purpose.

Love never falls out of its own character.

Love is fully mature in the measure of our acquiescence to it.

Love clarifies our vision and self–understanding, without destroying our uniqueness.

Love exceeds all other eternal things, its realizations being greater than faith, its desires greater than hope.

Agape love remains the essential character of Jesus. As we continue, may the pomegranates and golden bells of Aaron's blue robe remind us of those things we enjoy "in Christ." May He walk through the tabernacle of our being in His beauty.

## Joy (*chara*)

"The fruit of the Spirit is ... joy." As is the character of holy love, so is joy. Jesus said,

"These things I have spoken to you, that My joy may remain in you, and that your joy may be full" (John 15:11).

Joy is love's inebriation. The Apostle Peter described it in inebriating terms:

"... Though now you do not see Him, yet believing, you rejoice with joy inexpressible and full of glory ..." (1 Peter 1:8b).

"For these are not drunk, as you suppose, since it is only the third hour of the day. But this is what was spoken by the prophet Joel: 'And it shall come to pass in the last days, says God, that I will pour out of My Spirit on all flesh'" (Acts 2:15-17a).

What a natural consequence of our Lord's love, poured out into our hearts by the Holy Spirit! The Pentecost company, purged in heart, filled with God the Holy Spirit, tongues loosened to convey the gospel message to Jews on pilgrimage, seemed drunk with wine. Self–consciousness did not leave them, just that heavy anchor of fear that pulls the light vessel of the soul down into the deep waters of circumstance. In truth, they poured out of the Upper Room inebriated with the better wine of holiness, wine which awakens to soundness, not to foolishness; to clear speech, not to noisy slurs; to dignity, not to theatrical antics.

The word used to describe Peter's joy-filled message on that day emphasized honorable and orderly speaking. The word is *apophthengomai* and is found in Acts 2:4 ("utterance"), and Acts 2:14 ("said").

The Joy of Jesus was always in Him. He could never absent Himself from what He was. Though not always noticeable among men, it lay within, as close at hand as the grief and sorrow we have caused Him. Joy is more than an outward exhibition of smiles or laughter, though it does manifest these at times. It need not be entertained, neither does it need pep-rally gimmicks to exist. There is no evidence that Jesus ever lost control in laughter, but we could sense the quality of His humor by way of some of His parables. Yet in the fancies of our imagination, or even out of the influences of our culture we are bound to remember that this is the Son of God, doing and saying only what His Father commissioned, for the sake of a lost world. He has no self-gratifying agenda. He does not acquiesce to the feelings of the crowd. He is a perfectly balanced presence. His Word gives those guidelines, even for humor, natural to Him, to become natural to us as we know Him. He is not a hilarious Christ, and we are admonished toward His same inward control.

> "But fornication and all uncleanness or covetousness, let it not even be named among you, as is fitting for saints; Neither filthiness, nor foolish talking, nor coarse jesting, which are not fitting, but rather giving of thanks" (Ephesians 5:3,4).

No filthiness, no foolishness, no facetiousness—humor, yes, but clean and harmless.

In fact, the emphasis upon His life seems more toward sorrow, but even there, joy has not left Him. That is a daring assertion, but how often do we also find the deep reservoir of joy in the midst of testing? While sorrow weighs heavy, we can find holy joy afresh by resting prayerfully in His comforts.

Joy is often produced from the wine vat of crushing trials. How strange the ways of God! The saints who endure great trials imbibe in Christ to find the sweet richness of His wine. Real joy ages in wisdom and self-control. Though but a drop of heavenly joy touches the tongue of the new-born saint, enough to make one crave for more, understand that "God gives His wine in His time." It depends in some measure upon the season of our personal life. Our hearts "in Christ" become like a wine cellar. We do not escape to the "cellar," but take from its store in the company of the Holy Spirit that which makes our cup run over in the presence of our enemies.

This quality of God's love always remained with Jesus, and its rich flow without doubt could be seen in His countenance and heard deeply in His conversation. Love communion with Him develops His joy in us, beyond the contour of our lips.

### Peace (*eirene*)

"Peace I leave with you, My peace I give to you; not as the world gives do I give to you (John 14:27).

"For He Himself is our peace ... through the cross ..." (Ephesians 2:14-16).

"... the peace of God, which surpasses all understanding, will guard your hearts and minds through Christ Jesus ..." (Philippians 4:7).

"Now may the God of peace Himself sanctify you completely; and may your whole spirit, soul, and body be preserved blameless at the coming of our Lord Jesus Christ" (1 Thessalonians 5:23).

Jesus is our peace. Those are serene words, demonstrated extensively by Him as He ministered on earth. He commanded peace for a raging sea and raging souls. Ultimately and of greatest importance, He conquered raging sin through His cross.

"... the chastisement for our peace was upon him ..." (Isaiah 53:5).

The Apostle Paul illustrated that peace in Ephesians 2:14-18 with a few profound words: a "broken wall." He refers to an actual wall built in the temple court to separate Gentile from Jewish worshippers. For a Gentile to trespass would have brought the sentence of death. The wall symbolized Israel as more highly favored and superior to the Gentile world. As prophesied by the prophets of Israel, however, when Messiah appeared, even Gentiles would be drawn to God through Him. Israel would remain in His favored nation status, but spiritually, all mankind would have access to the Lord, because Christ broke down the separating wall.

Peace is "in His flesh," that is, in His humanity. His flesh was given "for the life of the world" (John 6:51). The God of peace is Jesus, who with His humanity meets our humanity, spirit, soul, and body—whoever we are—and works His peacemaking, His holy wholeness throughout every part of every part, that we may be ready to meet Him at His Parousia.

He becomes us. That is, He meets our disarray with His orderliness; our discord with His harmony. The idea of peace from Jesus relates to bringing us together personally, and on a grander and more difficult scale, to bring us together universally, i.e., to unite all believers, regardless of cultural, racial, social, intellectual, sexual differences (not preferences, but differences). Peace eliminates those distinctions, and places us on common ground, in Christ (Galatians 3:28). Peace from Jesus creates a holy culture, a new race of humanity, a distinct society, an intellect balanced by the mind of Christ, and is able to go beyond gender bias, according to the appointment of God the Holy Spirit.

His peace is "in one body through the cross." How amazingly mellow is the unity of a congregation in which the Lord is in fact Lord of all the congregants. When this Great Mediator between God and man becomes Mediator between man and man, the critical eye upon the extremes of human variations is replaced by love. No other entity on the face of the earth brings such divergence of personalities together as He does.

Within the framework of Paul's thought is the implication of sacrifice. Remember that our New Testament truths rise up from Hebrew roots. With that understanding, we see even better the prerequisite to our peace in the ancient customs of settling agreement between two opposing parties. Covenant was made through the sacrifice of an animal prepared for eating by both sides. As they ate, they were unified by participation in the body of the same animal.

The peace offering of Leviticus 3:1-17 parallels the offering of Jesus as the Lamb of God for sinners slain, and even its procedure applies to our Lord.

"... Aaron's sons shall burn it on the altar upon the burnt sacrifice, which is on the wood that is on the fire, a sweet aroma to the Lord" (Leviticus 3:5).

So much was occurring during the hours of our Lord's suffering, so much beyond the sight of those present. So much beyond our own grasp also, and often beyond our willingness to study it at length. The priestly ritual mandated perpetual daily offerings, perpetual bloodshed upon the great Bronze Altar, so that all day long, piece by piece, the vicarious sacrifices were kept burning. That is but representative of eternity's love gift poured into the limits of time in Jesus' Passion. He was there in full devotion to the Father's will. That was His "burnt/holocaust offering." Corresponding to the levitical ceremony, upon the wood of the Cross, rising through the fire of Jesus' total devotion appears His offering of peace, an aroma pleasing to God on behalf of man.

Peace is love's unification, the restoration of opposing forces and elimination of barriers. For us that first means that we have peace with God through Christ's crucifixion. More deeply it means that peace has us through our total devotion upon the altar of His will.

## Love, Joy, Peace

The Lord Jesus perfectly paradigmed these beautiful characteristics in the company of all men. An aura of manly grace balanced His stride and His speech before them. His pure heart poured forth an eloquence satiated and satiating with love's nature, love's inebriation, and love's unity. Before His Father in private, He cultivated this cluster of fruitfulness,

Christ's Character in the
Fruit of the Spirit

nourished it in His own soul, bathed it in His tears, and produced its evidence to the world. Love, joy, and peace having abounded in private prayer would naturally grow into other forms, such as in the two remaining clusters.

## Longsuffering (*makrothumia*)

This quaint old word distinguishes itself from what we call "patience." Both are used in the Bible, but a delineation between them exists, minor though it be. The following verse shows them used together, thus intending to show a degree of difference. Paul prayed that we might be

"... strengthened with all might, according to His glorious power, for all patience and longsuffering with joy ..." (Colossians 1:11).

" While patience is the temper which does not easily succumb under suffering, longsuffering is the self–restraint which does not hastily retaliate a wrong. The one is opposed to cowardice or despondency, the other to wrath or vengeance" *(Thayer Greek–English Lexicon of the New Testament).*

Longsuffering suffers long, like the wick of an oil lamp that lowly and slowly burns in accord with the extent of its saturation with the oil, or like a furnace flame under the control of a thermostat. It is love's fire that is ignited, but the flame consumes retaliation before it bums the antagonist.

A cadet classroom was set up in congregational form, with chairs divided into two sides, an aisle down the middle, and elbow room between each chair. A small piece of furniture became the "Holiness Table" and the lectern the pulpit. As the cadets entered, they were told to sit in their designated seats. As the lesson was taught, the theme became evident: the limits of your own space. "You have no right to pass over into space belonging to another, unless invited. To move in without invitation is a trespass," the teacher said. Some are more savvy than others concerning their interactive limitations. But many are not.

The emphasis was at least two–fold: individual space and individual trespass. Who has not been disturbed by the unmitigated air of some intrusive personality? A fire of temperament burns within us, and an undue "in your face" approach only kindles the flame. Some are aware of that, and by the sensitizing grace of God at work inwardly, know when to "back off." The fool walks on in flagrant violation of individual space, his overstep crushing the safety or courtesy that might have been cultivated. The man in whom dwells the Holy Spirit is enabled to keep his fires low, even when the "aggressor" intentionally or unintentionally passes beyond rightful borders.

Longsuffering makes a good psychologist, if borne as fruit of the Spirit. It has interest in another man's immortal soul, and desires to subdue its own temper while graciously sifting through the otherwise obnoxious behavior of an offender.

In the voice of Jesus, you can hear the cry of divine longsuffering for Jerusalem, as He laments over it in His last days on earth:

> "O Jerusalem, Jerusalem, the one who kills the prophets and stones those who are sent to her! How often I wanted to gather your children together, as a hen gathers her chicks under her wings, but you were not willing!" (Matthew 23:37).

Christ's Character in the
Fruit of the Spirit

Longsuffering is a trait that never ceases to long for the grace of God upon the one who causes the suffering or irritation.

## Gentleness (*chrestotes*)

Some translations read "kindness" instead of "gentleness." No need here to argue about words. My preference is "gentleness." The second characteristic of love in this cluster is also the central characteristic of love's fruit.

The prophet Isaiah foretold the gentleness of Messiah when he wrote,

> "He will feed His flock like a shepherd; He will gather the lambs with His arm, and carry them in His bosom, and gently lead those who are with young" (Isaiah 40:11).

> "A bruised reed He will not break, and smoking flax He will not quench ..." (Isaiah 42:3).

Gentleness stands like the capstone of a pyramid, or like the crown of a pillar, in its importance. The other fruit, like precise vertical lines in a column, lead up to, and down from, gentleness. Here is possibly the supreme trait of love, a kind spirit toward others.

Longsuffering should lead into gentleness. In fact, Paul says, "Love suffers long, and is kind [gentle] ..." (1 Corinthians 13:4).

Longsuffering burns by the oil of the Spirit within; gentleness blesses with the oil of the Spirit poured out upon others. Gentleness is love's unction. I knew a man whose gentleness was so strong that he would rather put himself in jail than cause harm to his wife. She very aggressively assaulted his Christianity. At times he would have visible bruises from her abuse. But his heart was deeply in love with his Master, and he bore the torment with a gentleness that knew no vengeance.

When in the company of Jesus harshness dissipates, gentleness precipitates. When in the company of one who has been with Jesus, the same is evident, perhaps because the gentle one has realized the contrast of his own former harshness as compared with the gentleness of God toward his own soul.

Commissioner Samuel Brengle wrote that upon seeing the humility of Jesus, he despised himself. Brengle, having the voice of a resonant orator and the knowledge of a seminarian, a man of holy living, baptized in the Holy Spirit, made gentle by the pure love of God, evidenced naturally that he had been with Jesus.

## Goodness (*agathosune*)

Goodness is love's benevolence. It is love's receivable gift. The first four characteristics of love's fruit really concern the believer's personal adjustment for fellowship with others, first to God, then to men. Gentleness displays the spirit of those adjustments. Goodness distributes the influence of those adjustments to others.

All of love's fruit savors of humbleness. Humbleness in God's presence allows for increase of His love, joy, and peace. Humbleness before God produces humbleness before men and toward men through longsuffering and gentleness. Humbleness develops from the realization that all one possesses has been freely received, and should be freely given.

"... And remember the words of the Lord Jesus, that He said, 'It is more blessed to give than to receive'" (Acts 20:35b).

What we are saying here is not limited to the realm of material things, though in this world of need, giving for the sustenance of others is a truly Judeo–Christian ethic. Goodness also includes the grace of listening, the openness of availability, the thoughtfulness of honest counsel, the tenderness of empathy. Who could better exemplify it than Jesus?

"Come to Me, all you who labor and are heavy laden, and I will give you rest. Take My yoke upon you and learn from Me, for I am gentle and lowly in heart, and you will find rest for your souls. For My yoke is easy and My burden is light" (Matthew 11:28-30).

The goodness of God leads us to repentance. It has as its aim the reconciliation of others to God. Goodness is an evangelist whose charities have interest in the present and future worlds. Jesus' material blessings—miracles of physical provision and restoration—had the ultimate aim of benefitting others with understanding of the kingdom of His Father. The fruit of goodness keeps temporality in tune with eternity.

## Faithfulness (*pistis*)

We come to the last cluster, which regards our intrapersonal relationship. It is not last in importance, for it branches out from the same Vine. Its grows alongside the other fruit and is enriched from the same soil of devotion and discipline. Pruned by the same Hand for flowering and flourishing, it yields to the Husbandman the same delightful satisfaction. God delights in the soul's restoration.

Faithfulness is love's loyalty. The King James Version used only the word "faith," because the Greek word is the same. Faith connotes belief that unfolds when we surrender to God; faithfulness is belief submitted to the world as proof, in keeping with a regenerated spirit.

Faithfulness trusts and is trustworthy. It is love's guardian of motives. It is also love's student of standards. Faithfulness is love's honor guard, love's conscience, love's immutability. It is loyal to the heaven–born life and the principals of its heaven–born nature—the nature of Jesus.

Faithfulness is the private investigator of the soul's scene. It is the Holy Spirit's implement for self–examination. It is like the gyroscope of a ship, keeping balance as the ship rolls from port to starboard in its watery path. It is the fruit of obedience to the law written upon the heart.

Jesus is called "Faithful and True" (Revelation 19:11). For our sanctification and preservation unto the Parousia of Christ Jesus, we are promised, "He who calls you is faithful, who also will do it" (1 Thessalonians 5:24).

## Meekness (*praotes*)

Meekness is love's brokenness, the surrendered will, the bondslave of love. Meekness is love stigmatized by the marks of Jesus. It carries about the dying of the Lord Jesus, so that the life of Jesus may be manifested through the tabernacle of our mortal flesh.

Its voice becomes our conscience, its vision becomes our thought. It is the anchor of our faithfulness, the guardian of our goodness, the sweetness of our gentleness, the conductor of our longsuffering, the threshold of our peace, the room of our joy, the table of our love.

Meekness is the harrowed ground that receives the grain of the Word and lives. Meekness conducts itself by wisdom from above. It is free from bitterness and boastfulness. The holiness of God as a witness remains in the heart in one who has been broken.

Jesus taught, "Blessed are the meek, for they shall inherit the earth" (Matthew 5:5). What did He mean by this paradox? How can one so broken and humiliated, so unsuccessful and of low esteem inherit the earth which has ravaged him? Jesus said, "Come and learn of Me ..." Come to where we know Him best. Come often, stay long, bow down, surrender before His cross. A glimpse of Him there, all for me, breaks the heart and opens the floodgates of blessing. That can only happen where meekness is cultivated.

How shall the meek inherit the earth? That is a promise of things to come ultimately. For the present age, as the world sees it, the submissive, passive, unaspiring, nonbelligerent man or woman has no life. That world view consists mainly of judgment by exterior appearances and adoration of short–lived heroes who must finally realize the temporality and ignominy of their fame. They inherit nothing in eternity. The meek, though unknown, overlooked, and disdained in their present condition, will inherit all things good. They taste it in their hearts, touch it by faith, rejoice for it in their words, because they know the fruition of brokenness. They have seen it in the Lord.

## Self–Control (*enkrateia*)

This characteristic is love's mysticism. It is like the mystic priest who contemplates and concentrates upon his inward functions and purposes. Self–control actually means "inner control." It does not live on the surface, or merely in the realm of the body, though the body becomes subject to its discipline. It is the wise and knowledgeable trainer of souls.

It gives focus to the inward exercises of thought. It helps the emotion and intellect to come together to fulfill life's personal vocation. It reinforces the will to restrain from doing unprofitable things, and to constrain to do what is profitable. It chooses not only the good, but the excellent. Because it is allied to all the other fruit, its character is grounded in love. Its precise work is accomplished in love. It self-examines, under the scrutiny of the Holy Spirit. The Spirit helps trim away the fat of criticism and hypocrisy and builds the muscles of truth and discipline. The Holy Spirit who enables for "inner control" in the Christian, empowers for "outer control."

As though He were the Divine Mechanic, He reaches down into our complicated human parts of soul and spirit, repairs the faulty engine of imagination, restores the drive to run smoothly, and steers our way through the traffic of other souls not for our own safety alone, but for others as well. We become a vehicle fit for His use.

Inner–control literally means "inner strength" (*enkrateia: en +kratos*), the kind of strength that masters the art and science of its subject. It is love's domination in life's deter-minations, especially when those decisive moments come for our participation with other saints "in Christ." The Corinthians needed that aspect of love as they exercised the Gifts of the Spirit—and so do we, like the fruit among the bells of Aaron's robe.

Christ's Character in the
Fruit of the Spirit

What have these characteristics to do with the Hebrew Tabernacle? Everything. From the fruit of the True Vine comes the Libation Wine. Like the libations of daily offerings, love is a life outpoured in sacrifice. Standing before the Ancient Tent was the Great Altar of Sacrifice. At its base lamb's blood was mingled with drink offerings of wine.

> "Now this is what you shall offer on the altar: two lambs of the first year, day by day continually. One lamb you shall offer in the morning, and the other lamb you shall offer at twilight. With one lamb shall be one–tenth of an ephah of flour mixed with one–fourth of a hin of pressed oil, and one–fourth of a hin of wine as a drink offering. And the other lamb you shall offer at twilight; and you shall offer with it the grain offering and the drink offering, as in the morning, for a sweet aroma, an offering made by fire to the Lord" (Exodus 29:38-41).

Blood and wine? The blood of a lamb and the blood of a vine? Yes. Not only life, but life abundant! "I am come that they may have life, and that they may have it more abundantly" (John 10:10b).

We had no life until He gave us His life. He is the True Lamb and the True Vine together, the fruit of each symbolizing His outpoured life unto death in His atoning blood. Atonement and abundance form the full purpose of His life given for us. The evidence that these graces have taken effect in personal life is the fruit of the Spirit.

> The fruit of the Spirit is holy, like the sacredness of holy places.
> The fruit of the Spirit is righteous, like the orderliness and decency of worship.

The fruit of the Spirit is heavenly, like the angelic tapestry of the sanctuary.

The fruit of the Spirit is beautiful, like the instruments of sanctuary ministry.

The fruit of the Spirit is glorious, like the illuminating flames of the Menorah.

The fruit of the Spirit is nourishing, like the bread of fellowship.

The fruit of the Spirit is mediatorial, like the fragrance of incense.

The fruit of the Spirit is covenantal, like the ark of the Law.

The fruit of the Spirit is merciful, like the propitiatory lid

The fruit of the Spirit is the character of Jesus.

Remember that Aaron could not enter the holy places without the symbols of his ministry, pomegranates alternating with golden bells. The bells were to sound, but not against each other. That would have been intolerable. They needed the cushioning of pomegranates to temper their ringing. Nor would pomegranates alone be approved. They needed the accompanying sound of the bells—just enough of one and just enough of the other to walk in holy places.

We are accepted by the heavenly Father only through the character of Christ. The Father is pleased with those who bear His Son's likeness, and that likeness is found in the fruit of the Spirit. The fruit of the Spirit, by divine plan, will always give proper intonation to the gifts of the Spirit. The one speaks of His character, the other speaks of His charisma.

# Christ's Charisma in the Gifts of the Spirit

The Gifts of the Spirit receive attention mostly in chapters twelve through fourteen of 1 Corinthians. Chapter twelve lists nine gifts; chapter thirteen compares and correlates them with love; chapter fourteen lays down the principles for exercising gifts.

Paul described the Corinthian setting and the corrections he had to make among those believers. He illustrated the operation of gifts from the Holy Spirit in terms of a body, each gift having its peculiar and necessary function. Other epistles of Paul and Peter also list gifts, but the basic ones seem to be given in the Corinthian letter.

They are called "the gifts of the Spirit" or the *charismata* of the Spirit, charismata simply meaning "gifts." From the word *charis* (gift) comes the term "charismatic" (giftedness). Today a person described as charismatic is considered attractive, gregarious, and influential. Generally it speaks of the magnetic power of a leader, whether in the affairs of business or entertainment. But in the Bible, every Christian is a charismatic person. Every true member of a fellowship of believers has a gift from God to use for the benefit of the others.

With most of us, the gift may lay dormant. Nonetheless, it is there, and it can be found through prayer and fellowship, and can be certified by others whose hearts are right with God. Evidence of its genuineness will be seen in its effectiveness in the lives of others, for the Holy Spirit gives His gifts for the building up of the body, ultimately to transform the

If used in love, the Gifts of the Spirit in accord with love, show themselves "... in all goodness, righteousness, and truth" (Ephesians 5:9).

body into the likeness of Jesus Christ.

In the book of Exodus, within the context of chapters twenty–five through forty, chosen men and women were endued by the Holy Spirit to construct the sacred intricacies of the Tabernacle. He gave them unction for their tasks, and the result was a center of worship, salvation, holiness, and service to God for men. We have already described and defined the physical Tabernacle and some of its rituals, but in New Testament revelation we know of whom its pattern speaks—our Lord Jesus Christ first; then us as we are placed in Him. Every church is meant to be His representative body. That should render inoperative any attempt to compete with our brethren who congregate in other fellowships. The idea is not to be bigger and better than any other "church" in town. The aim is to be all that God the Holy Spirit wills to make of each body. Though the outreach to save souls should always be active, the central thrust is to seek the Lord's formative power in the body of Christ. The church body may not always be growing in numbers, but the church body should always grow spiritually. Growth is not always physical, but it is always visible—and so is non–growth, deterioration, and death.

Churches die not by of lack of programmatic activity but by lack of spiritual activity. The Holy Spirit will not abandon the church that responds to His leading. But He will not give charisma to a church that plans its strategies apart from His leading. Here we test the spirits by the Bible, for the Lord will do nothing apart from His Word. The question should remain before us, "What does the Scripture say?" Otherwise we could easily follow error in doctrine and practice, and false leaders who "have a way with" us. If we meet and part without having known more about Jesus, and more about ourselves from His Word, we have met in vain. It has become, as Paul says, "... a form of godliness, but denying its power" (2 Timothy 3:5).

A form is but the outward appearance. We do have formation. The Holy Spirit rules by orderliness and decency. But His formation among us involves His power, power that enriches each life present in the quality of our Christlikeness. His holy work need not, must not conform to this world. His work is altogether different. His manifestation in each one of us is certified by how much of Jesus can be seen through the exercise of our place in His body. The Gifts of the Spirit are *charismata* to do what Jesus would do; the Fruit of the Spirit are characteristics by which to perform the *charismata* as Jesus would perform them. One may indeed have many gifts, and use them without love. If we are honest, we will know what is love–bound and what is not. But we cannot use the gifts legitimately without love. Otherwise, the assembly becomes but an empty, useless show. But if used in love, the Gifts of the Spirit in accord with love show themselves "... in all goodness, righteousness, and truth" (Ephesians 5:9).

Use these criteria to discern the true from the erroneous, and real blessing will be given.

## Gift Categories

An important technicality exists in the Corinthian gifts which grammatically divides them into three distinct groups. A difference in the use of two words separates the gifts definitively and functionally. Those two words are translated into one English word, the word "other" (or "an other"). The Greek words are *allos* (one/another of the same kind), and *heteros* (one/another of a different kind). Ally, alliance, alloy, and allegory are kindred to *allos*. Heterodoxy and heterogeneous use *heteros* as a differentiating prefix.

Both of these words are used in the list of the Gifts of the Spirit, and their significance might be better understood through the following paraphrase of 2 Corinthians 12:

> ... the Spirit of God manifests Himself through each believer in ways that benefit all believers. One person receives through the Holy Spirit *the reasoning of wisdom*; to another (*allos* = another of the same kind) by the same Holy Spirit *the reasoning of knowledge*;
>
> to another (*heteros* = another of a different kind) *faith* by the same Holy Spirit; to another (*allos* = another recipient of the same kind as the preceding gift of faith) gifts of healings; to another (*allos*) working of miracles; to another (*allos*) prophecy; to another (*allos*) discerning of spirits;
>
> to another (*heteros* = another of a different kind) *kinds of tongues*; to another (*allos* = another of the same kind of gift which preceded it) *interpretation of tongues*.

A study of that division leads to the following conclusion:

        I. *Theological Gifts*
                A. A Word/Reasoning of Wisdom
                B. A Word/Reasoning of Knowledge
       II. *Ecclesiological Gifts*
                A. Faith

Shadow and Substance

        B. Gifts of Healings

        C. Working of Miracles

        D. Prophecy

        E. Discerning of Spirits

III. *Glossological Gifts*

        A. Kinds of Tongues

        B. Interpretation of Tongues

During the first year of the Exodus, Moses was receiving God's system of beliefs (theology), God's order of worship for the people of Israel (ecclesiology) where tongues were present, according to Hebrews 2:3; 12:18,19, and His method of speaking His Word through angels (glossology). The purpose of such manifestations from the Lord to Moses and then to the people centers upon His desire to dwell among His people.

As Israel in type and location became that dwelling place, the Church uniquely realizes His dwelling in every place it congregates all over the world.

## The Theological Gifts

*Wisdom*

"A word of wisdom" and "a word of knowledge" by nature run together. They do not represent some spontaneous revelation concerning an ailment or material necessity. That properly belongs to the next category. These are doctrinal gifts. Both are introduced by "a word," a *logos*. In the common use *logos* indicates reasoned thought expressed through speaking, or speaking as a result of reasoned thought. Wisdom and knowledge, as gifts of the Spirit, are enablements for the reasoning of theological matters. They together build the foundation of our beliefs. They are the forgers of church dogma, the scribes of the sacred biblical testaments. They show what is right to believe, reveal the inter–testamental connections, and indicate what is right to practice. They filter out errors from the truth. They are the harmonizers of our faith, the defenders of Christ's being and work.

I see them operating in the law of Moses. I also see them illustrated in the Urim and Thummim carried by Aaron the first high priest of Israel. The Urim and Thummim were consulted for direction when major decisions arose, and have been interpreted as "lights and perfections." The Urim and Thummim of the New Testament can be easily described as wisdom and knowledge. Wisdom's lights give revelation of holy truth; the perfections of knowledge give framework for their expression (Exodus 28:30).

These two gifts are first found in Christ Jesus, "... in whom are found all the treasures of wisdom and knowledge" (Colossians 2:3).

Wisdom itself is not only a charism of the Son of God. Jesus is Wisdom personified. He gave Himself that designation in two different places in the course of His preaching. He presents a statement given by "the wisdom of God" (Luke 11:49-51). He repeats the statement, identifying the voice of God and His own as synonomous (Matthew 23:34-36). That correlates well with Proverbs 8:12-31.

We should find also that every gift is a manifestation of Jesus' powers. Each, then, should be used as He would use them, for they are His personal possessions, entrusted to us.

In Jesus' parable of the talents (Matthew 25:14-30), the "goods" of the man who was going to absent himself from his servants for a while are represented by the "talents." We know that Jesus speaks of Himself there, distributing to His servants portions of His property. "And to one He gave five talents, to another two, and to another one, to each according to his own ability ..." (Matthew 25:15).

We know the story well, and its interpretation has been varied. The talents are given to each servant according to his own ability, and the expectation of the master upon returning is for profit. As with the talents, so with the gifts. First, they are of Christ and belong to Him; they are "His goods." Second, they are only entrusted to us and must be used actively and profitably. Third, they must be presented to Him with increase when He returns. The increase represents the investment of those gifts in the activities of our service for the Lord. Each gift is given according to the measure of our individual ability to use them. He expects no more, no less. That should provoke diligence for our accountability, awe for the beauty of the gifts, and reverence in the use of them because we know their sacred Source. We also know of that price paid by Jesus Himself that He might distribute to mere men and women that which belongs to Him, our Sovereign Lord.

"But to each one of us grace was given according to the measure of Christ's gift. Therefore He says: 'When He ascended on high, He led captivity captive, and gave gifts to men.' (Now this, 'He ascended'—what does it mean but that He also descended into the lower parts of the earth? He who descended is also the One who ascended far above all the heavens, that He might fill all things)" (Ephesians 4:7-9).

Wisdom and knowledge likely pertain to those offices given in 1 Corinthians 12:26, especially apostles, prophets, and teachers.

"Who is wise and understanding among you? Let him show by good conduct that his works are done in the meekness of wisdom ...

The wisdom that is from above is first pure, then peaceable, gentle, willing to yield, full of mercy and good fruits, without partiality, without hypocrisy" (James 3:13,17).

## The Ecclesiological Gifts

*Faith*

Stephen, the first martyr of the Church and one of the first deacons, was "a man full of faith and of the Holy Spirit" and "full of faith and power" (Acts 6:5,8). His was persuasive faith, for he was fully convinced of the truth of the gospel of Jesus Christ. His faith was so complete that the power of the Holy Spirit worked mightily through him in his debates with his opponents.

"They were not able to resist the wisdom and the Spirit by which he spoke" (Acts 6:10).

Stephen would have the status of a layperson in today's Church, but note the other enablements divinely given to him: "He did great wonders and signs," for he was full of the

Holy Spirit to whom Stephen's gift of faith was committed. Layman? Yes! A place of subjection to the apostles' positions, a place of servitude in the Church, but whose gift was as important as any in the function of the Church. In the early Church, as seen with Stephen, and later with Philip, the Lord used whom He would, beyond the office of the specially ordained leaders.

Faith is always that "substance of things hoped for, the evidence of things not seen." (Hebrews 11:1) By it through grace we are saved, and by it we continue in the salvation experience. At whatever level faith is working, it essentially believes that beyond the visible world there lay at hand the invisible world of God's power, to bring about things thought impossible by mere men. The charism of faith is the gift to believe beyond the circumstances.

We each have our measure of faith by which to walk, but some have been enabled with special measures of great faith to believe in answers to needs on behalf of the people of God. These are men and women of vision and prayer, persons who can move mountains, who walk in such optimism for the spiritual power available, that what is lacking to the sight of most of us is seen by them as already supplied. They are like Elisha, who prayed that his servant's eyes be opened to behold the protective presence of God's army.

Such a gift is still needed, such individuals are yet important to the existence of the Church, especially in those ever increasing parts of the world where the Church faces great opposition. I suppose that for many churches this gift lacks exercise, because in our part of the world we have more than we need. Our leisure and prosperity gives faith a paradoxical opportunity for the awakening of the Church. Draw aside just one man to believe fervently, without a shadow of doubt, into the fellowship of prayer, and God will "move in" to answer faith's groanings. The man or woman who perceives this to be true may well have the gift of faith. They can freely pray like Elijah for an awakening drought or for a reviving rain, both in outward nature, and in the ominous realms of spiritual encounters. The one gifted in this way can with quietness and simplicity just believe, and God rewards.

## Gifts of Healing

Some strange methods were used for healing in the Old Testament. Those complainers in the wilderness sojourn looked toward a bronze serpent on a pole, and they were healed of snake bites received because of their insubordination. For a leper to have certification of cleansing, two small birds were used in a peculiar ritual (Leviticus 13,14). One of the birds was killed in a container of special water, and the remaining bird was tied alive to a piece of cedar wood with a scarlet cord and hyssop. The living bird was then dipped into the blood of the dead one. With the living bird still bound to the cedar and hyssop, the priest sprinkled blood upon the leper seven times for his healing. Then the bird was let go, to fly away over an open field—yet stained with the blood into which it had been dipped.

Leprosy was real. Healing was real. They both had messianic significance. Leprosy physically portrays what sin is spiritually. The birds portray Jesus, His death, and resurrection. His blood is the source from which comes all of our healing and the gifts of healing. It is crucial that we keep in mind that this also is an expression of Jesus' powers, not ours. He Himself is in the provision.

"Gifts" and "healings" are used in the plural, implying a variety of healings, in line with the idiosyncrasies of our humanity. Emotions often need healing. Some can comfort with non–threatening, non–invasive counsel. Bodies need healing: some can by a touch and prayer restore the sick to health. Intellect needs healing: some are enabled to correct wrong reasoning, or to give further health to those with limited understanding of the truth. Social interaction often needs healing: some have the gift of mediating for the sake of peaceful reconciliation. If any of these are truly a gift from the Spirit of God, Christ–honoring success will result, the recipient will have victorious restoration, and the one gifted will seek no personal recognition.

Healing was a tremendous part of Jesus' ministry. It yet has its place, for sickness of some kind afflicts us all at some time or another. However, for any number of examples which could be presented, healing is not always granted. Somehow this too is considered in the purposes of God to be fulfilled, and those purposes may never be understood this side of heaven. Consider Job, Paul, Epaphroditus, Timothy, the many saints throughout history, and those deeply godly ones living today who suffer ailments for a lifetime. We cannot say that healing will occur in this life to everyone who is a Christian; nor can we say lack of faith leaves you in your infirmity. Remember that there are healthy sinners as well. Are they healthy because of salvation? Not at all. Our favor with God goes deeper than the body. The body is but a vehicle through which our Lord performs His ministry as He will. He knows the total picture of our condition, and how we may best be used of Him for the sake of others. He also knows in what condition we may best conform to the image of His Son. And His Son suffered. The richest knowledge of Him often comes at the point of suffering.

The gift of healing is yet valid and operating, but only in concert with the Holy Spirit's appointments. Certainly the Bible teaches of healing, that the united prayers of two

Christ's Charisma in the
Gifts of the Spirit

or three will be answered. What the answer is depends upon His will. If it is not His will, who would want it? And such praying, done in Jesus' name, will have Jesus' mind, and therefore will be offered up to God with Jesus' sensitivities. And the gifts of healings will have Jesus' touch.

## Working of Miracles

Miraculous powers belong especially to the offices of prophet and apostle. But in the Church, such power has place with whom the Holy Spirit chooses.

A miracle, to our thinking, is an intervention into natural processes for the sake of supplying a need. Jesus performed innumerable miracles. The motivation for His miracles was compassion. They also served as signs of of His messiahship. John the Baptist asked from his prison cell, "Are you the Coming One, or do we seek another?" In the moments John's messengers brought the question to Jesus, He performed several miraculous works as evidence He was the Christ.

> "... Go and tell John the things which you hear and see: the blind see and the lame walk; the lepers are cleansed and the deaf hear; the dead are raised up and the poor have the gospel preached to them" (Matthew 11:4,5).

*Dunamis*, or miracle, occurs when *energeia* or energy/work issues from God through that chosen one into the prevailing circumstance. Healing, the gift discussed previously, is called a miracle, so a distinction should be made between that and the gift of miraculous power. To that distinction other works of Jesus would more exemplify the gift at hand. He

Shadow and Substance

calmed a raging sea at least twice. He supplied bread and fish at least twice. He provided tax money once. He manifested His glory once in a great transformational display, and in measure at other times (John 2:11). Jesus Himself was a walking miracle, considering the virgin birth and how His life was preserved. Until His predetermined hour had come, no one could harm Him (John 2:4; 7:6,8,30; 8:20; 12:23,27; 13:1; 17:1).

The miraculous was first demonstrated by the Lord Himself in the creation of all things out of no things. The sustaining of all things by the Son of God's word of power remains an ongoing miracle. His personal involvement universally is a miracle. His historical guidance for His people Israel is a continuing miracle. His personal intimacy within the hearts of all true believers is indeed a miracle. His formation of congregations as a part of His body is a marvelously miraculous gathering. And, if the conditions and timing are right and the need is at hand, someone, or perhaps several present, should manifest the gift of miracles, not in a circus display of power, but humbly, yes even anonymously, if possible. Perhaps that happens more often than we know.

Miracles are processes fast–forwarded in nature, or provisions that seem to come out of nowhere. They include protection from evil intentions and directions of will and emotion, thought and speech. They have visible manifestations and invisible operations, and they belong to the Church, and to Israel, as to no other people.

It must be remembered that in the last days, Satan and his cohorts will also work miracles, just as Pharaoh's men did in the presence of Moses and Aaron. But their powers were limited, and those miracles done by God's men prevailed. Discernment is needed to distinguish the true from the false, and God has given us a gift for that also.

Christ's Charisma in the
Gifts of the Spirit

# Prophecy

Prophets seem to come in seasonal waves. Isaiah's parable of the Beloved's Vineyard (Isaiah 5) is elaborated upon by Him who gave it to Isaiah, the Lord Jesus in His passion week (Matthew 21:33-46). Many individual prophets have appeared from the beginning of human history—Enoch, Noah, Abraham, Joseph, Moses, Samuel, Nathan, and others. They comprised the first wave of prophets, what some may call "the former prophets."

During the years of Israel's and Judah's demise, another great wave of prophetic flow was sent to the inhabitants to warn of impending danger, admonish against sin, and encourage the people concerning the distant future. Prophets were sent to examine and give a report on the condition of the vineyard God had planted. Those prophets were maligned and ill-treated. Then God sent His Son, the Heir of the vineyard, whom the inhabitants rejected, cast out, and killed.

This same Jesus said that we also would drink of His cup, because we are His prophets who bear testimony:

"... worship God! For the testimony of Jesus is the spirit of prophecy" (Revelation 19:10).

Even our witness to God's truth is of a prophetic nature. That is to say, for prophecy to be genuine it must have as its theme and purpose the glory of our Lord Jesus Christ. Anything less is false, self-gratifying, and dangerous.

The gift of prophecy refers to special power to forth-tell the gospel message, as in preaching. Expounding Scripture after the manner of a divinely sent announcer, this "town crier" alerts citizens of news good or bad. Paul says, "But he who prophesies speaks edification and exhortation and comfort to men" (1 Corinthians 14:3).

Prophecy is also a gift of foretelling. Its message comes through illumination in prayer, and the one God leads as His instrument understands that the message has a sense of urgency. In the first days of the Church, often more than one person would at any given time prophesy in the course of the meeting. It was not an exercise of competition, but rather a moving of the Holy Spirit upon those chosen to do so.

That exercise, for most, would probably be unacceptable today. An hour is sufficient! But if the interest is there, eternity steps into the borders of our time, and we are blessed beyond temporal limitations. As with every gift, God must lead.

## Discerning of Spirits

Though this gift is listed last in this section on Eccelesiatical gifts, it is certainly not the least. This gift assures the genuineness of all the other gifts.

Discerning of spirits may not only identify which person genuinely practices a gift. It also judges the motives behind the use of any gift. It is possible to have a legitimate gift and to use it illegitimately. That is why Paul inserted 1 Corinthians 13, the love chapter, to make sure "the hem of the garment" in the Holy Places rang with bells whose sound was tempered by the fruit of finely woven pomegranates.

Jesus could perceive the intentions of the heart, even read the thoughts of the minds of those who came to Him. Having such power, He was always in control of their inquiries. They may have asked one thing, but He knew their motives. Sometimes He re–directed their thoughts to more important things, as with Nicodemus. Sometimes He responded surprisingly forcefully, for He Himself was Truth and must by nature correct error, as with Peter in His confession and his misinterpretation of the Messiah's cross–bearing mission:

> "Jesus began to explain to the disciples that He must go to Jerusalem and suffer many things at the hands of the elders, chief priests and teachers of the law, and that He must be killed and on the third day be raised to life.
>
> "Peter took Him aside and began to rebuke Him. 'Never, Lord!' he said. 'This shall never happen to You!'
>
> "Jesus turned and said to Peter, 'Out of My sight, Satan! You are a stumbling block to Me; you do not have in mind the things of God, but the things of men'" (Matthew 16:21-23).

Shadow and Substance

He who has the gift of discerning spirits has an awesome responsibility. Correction, rebuke, and re–direction must be exercised with great humility. Arrogance has no place in its character. At the same time, boldness is required, boldness under the yoke of Christ, whose reproofs were given with the pangs of love. We absolutely need those who are divinely enabled to discern the spirits. This is not intuitive, but revelatory. It is not a mere supposition, but a clear understanding, and is to be exercised in a right spirit.

> "Brethren, if a man is overtaken in any trespass, restore such a one in a spirit of

gentleness, considering yourself lest you also be tempted" (Galatians 6:1).

## The Gift of Different Kinds of Tongues

This is probably the most difficult of the gifts, and the most abused (though all of the gifts have been abused here or there). I have heard tongues of the ecstatic sort. As a boy, before my teenage years, I went with my mother to The Salvation Army in the mornings, and with my father to a Pentecostal church at night. I learned from both, and have no desire to compare the denominations. Sometimes what I heard in tongues at the end of the Pentecostal meetings was beautiful, though I did not understand. I went to a college for one semester for Bible studies, and speaking in tongues ocurred in almost every general session to begin the day. Two other Christians and I felt a bit out of place. Those meetings had a peculiar start and an abrupt end, followed by what seemed to be an atmosphere completely unrelated in content or spirit to the preceding tongues spoken by nearly everyone at the same time. But I cannot deny, though I have never experienced that blessing, that there is a gift of tongues for the body of believers. Like any gift, it must be used with diligence and prayer.

What is this gift? First Corinthians 13:1 probably has the most accurate and concise description: "Though I speak with the tongues of men and of angels, but have not love, I have become as sounding brass or a clanging cymbal."

No need would have arisen to even mention "angel tongues" had it not referred to the language of angels. Nothing else leads up to the subject. I have thought at times that those two glossological classifications could imply eloquence (men) and ecstacy (angels). But that is a "gloss" over the clear writing, a denominational hermeneutic. The text means what it says. The experiences of many verify the authenticity of that kind of tongue. The whole phrase involves kind, genre, or genus. Human tongues are one genus; angelic tongues are another genus. The plural form, "kinds," suggests this.

The biblical accounts also suggest this, principally in the Book of Acts. In Acts 2:1-13, before Peter's message, the approximately one hundred and twenty believers were baptized in the Holy Spirit. They who hid in fear for their new belief were now empowered to tell about it. Those who listened to them thought they were drunk, an implication of ecstasy; others took seriously the astounding fact that these backward Nazarenes had spoken perfectly in languages they had not known before. The event was the Day of Pentecost. Pilgrim Jews from other lands heard the believers speak in their own familiar tongues. It was Babylon reversed. The electricity of God's mighty power held their attention while they listened, until Peter stood to preach. Then their thoughts were riveted upon Peter's words about the death and resurrection of Jesus Christ our Lord.

Those human tongues were manifested in other accounts as well:

The Samaritan Experience: tongues not mentioned but something was seen which evidenced a response of some kind from the believing Samaritans. It was also altogether something unmistakably twofold (Acts 8:1-13; 14-25).

Cornelius' Experience: he and his household, to that point at least "God-fearers," now were immersed in the Holy Spirit, and they spoke in tongues. What kind? It does not say. It does record that this "baptism" came before their "water baptism," and implies that the last act was probably a sprinkling or a pouring.

The Ephesian Experience: they were called believers/disciples, but who were followers of John the Baptist. Upon being baptized in Jesus' name, no doubt because now they believed in Jesus, they received the baptism of the Holy Spirit. Then they spoke in tongues and prophesied.

This is not to say that tongues are a necessity for salvation. It means that on occasions, in the early Church at least, upon receiving Christ as Savior and subsequently receiving the baptism in the Holy Spirit, some spoke in tongues. Those tongues and the gift of tongues, I believe, are not the same, though the possibility remains. But the gift of tongues applies to "body function" in an assembly of believers for believers; Pentecost tongues apply to a sign for unbelievers (human languages for the most part). Both may involve eloquence and ecstacy. Neither have lost their value. Both yet have place in Christian service as in centuries past. They are considered a part of the body, and a complete body would yet need this part. The probability is that for the misuse of the gift, or because of doubt concerning it, or fear of using it, it has not had the widespread application as it might otherwise have had. Cautiously we ask, "Do all speak with tongues?" The answer is, "No."

## Interpretation of Tongues

This must be the "grammarian" of the gifts of the Holy Spirit. It is the gift of hermeneutics, one who interprets the language spoken. What a gift some have for interpreting the deep thinking of Christian scholars, preachers, and teachers. What a gift to some whose minds are so enlightened that they can relay and decipher the angelic message given to another brother or sister. This is the gift required to be present when anyone speaks in another tongue. Years ago I heard someone say, "No wonder our people are confused today, when our choirs sing in Latin, and our preachers preach in Hebrew and Greek." Whatever unknown expression is presented in the congregation, interpretation must be given for the edification of those present. Clarity must be the aim. Conviction and consecration will be the result.

Commissioner Samuel Brengle wrote of some people's depth as being nothing more than mud puddles. If the Holy Spirit is revered as the Administrator of the congregation, inevitably light will be given.

## Conclusion

The Gifts of the Spirit are functions of the body of Christ, therefore they are powers that come from Him, to be used for Him in His ministry among us. They are His "Charisma." The Fruit of the Spirit are manifestations of His "Character." We can have the gifts without exercising them in love. That's a danger. We can have the Fruit without demonstration of the Gifts. That is no problem. The ideal is the presence of the gifts, as the Holy Spirit appoints their use. If He controls them, they will work in love.

Remember the Parable of the Talents? One servant took the portion of his Master's treasure he was entrusted with and hid it in the dirt. His act was of the flesh, not the Spirit. His excuse was a lie about his Master being unfair and capricious. When we appear before Christ, we will but recount before Him the lives we have lived. The thoughts of our hearts will re–surface, the explanations will but echo our character and reveal the way we have used and abused our charisma.

Shadow and Substance

May we have increase of our charisma through "transaction," the spiritual increase that comes through wise and active exercise of the entrusted gifts. This comes through prayerful and devoted use, especially in the body of Christ our Lord.

Christ's Charisma in the
Gifts of the Spirit

# Appendices

# The Oracle

Paraphrase of John 1:1-5,9,14,16,18

The Oracle forever was, and in that uncreated sphere
He forever was face to face with God,
and He Himself also
was God.
The same Oracle was with God when all things created began.
All things created were His work, and not one created thing
came into being without His thorough involvement.
In the Oracle was essential life,
and that life was the source of human illumination.
And that illumination always casts its revealing beams
into creation's darkness,
and though darkness made an attempt to do so,
it could not bring that illuminating power
under its control.

That was the fully perfect Illumination which
brings revelation to every man entering into the world.

Shadow and Substance

And the Oracle entered into His earthly sanctuary,
pitching His tabernacle among us,
and we gazed at times upon His excellent splendor,
such brilliance as could only come from One
related to God through Divine Sonship.
Such a manifestation was characterized by
gracious move and unerring speech.
And of such an array of His character we have been
and continue to be recipients,
growing through one gracious measure
of His life after another.

No one has ever seen God at any time
by his mere created vision.
The uniquely born Son of God (The Oracle),
the One who is forever in His Father's heart,
He alone has given accurate interpretation
of Him.

# A Word about Israel

Every truly Christian message has its roots in Israel's past, its trunk in her present, and its branches in her future.

I am not a "super–sessionist." I believe in the legitimacy of the Church as God's spiritual instrument in this era of history, but I also believe in the continuing legitimacy of Israel. The Church is not an entity that has superseded Israel; that is, we who belong to the Church have not taken her place. Both are current undeniable bodies; both in the world, but not of the world. The doubt sometimes expressed is that God does not have two kingdom programs running at the same time. Why not? The evidence is overwhelming that He does, scripturally and historically.

Israel may not be considered God's spiritual instrument at present, but according to proclamations from both Testaments, she is guaranteed a permanent favored place in divine plans. The covenant assured to Abraham, Isaac, and Jacob seemed void while the Hebrews were slaves in Egypt, though in the mysterious foreknowledge of God, His advance notice to Abraham promised them deliverance. Her liberation came after four hundred years, after hesitations and impediments, but it did come.

After forty years of wilderness probation, Moses prophesied the worldwide diaspora of the Jews, which actually began with invasions by Assyria, then Babylon, and stands today as a result of Rome's carnage of Jerusalem and its temple. But her history would not con-summate in her annihilation—either physically or spiritually. Although she seems that way to some, she is yet greatly beloved of God.

Jeremiah, the weeping prophet who lamented Jerusalem's destruction and warned of imminent captivity, scatters his messages of doom among God's promises of mercy and reclamation. God cannot and will not forget His covenant with His beloved Abraham.

> "Thus says the Lord, who gives the sun for a light by day, the ordinances of the moon and the stars for a light by night, who disturbs the sea, and its waves roar (the Lord of hosts is His name):

> "'If those ordinances depart from before Me,' says the Lord, 'then the seed of Israel shall also cease from being a nation before Me forever.'

> "Thus says the Lord: 'If heaven above can be measured, and the foundation of the earth searched out beneath, I will also cast off all the seed of Israel for all that they have done,' says the Lord" (Jeremiah 31:35-37).

Isaiah, the eloquent oracle, speaks often of Israel's latter day status, promising in detail her "second" return to her land, and the consequent glory to be manifested visibly there. "It shall come to pass in that day that the Lord shall set His hand again the second time to recover those who remain of His people who are left from [the North and South, East and West, and around the world] ... from the four corners of the earth" (Isaiah 11:11,12).

The first return of Israel to her land was by a small number of Jews. They remained in the land about five hundred years. Rome and many other nations scattered them and per-secuted them for centuries, but they now return "the second time" in a continuous flow to the land. Even before the present return, they maintained identity in every land. Had they been any other people, they would have disappeared, in light of their historically adverse cir-cumstances.

It is strange that those who accept the literal prophecies of Jesus' first advent reject the literality of His second advent. Suddenly, for them, all Scripture vaporizes into a so-called spiritual hermeneutic, and dangerously results in wind-blown opinions. We have no right to "individual interpretation." We who believe in Messiah's literal second coming must believe in Israel's second return to her land. To ignore that truth is willful blindness.

The Apostle Paul confirms in Romans 9–11 Israel's validity as a special people, not cast off from God's favor, but guaranteed a "re–grafting" when "the fullness of the Gentiles has come in" (Romans 11:17-33). The Apostle John sees Israel in varied ways in the Apocalypse (Revelation 7-14). The Apostle Matthew records Jesus Himself prophesying of Israel's latter day experience (Matthew 24,25). Wonderful exposition could be made upon such passages, and Israel would clearly yet be seen as God's elect people.

Hosea, the loving husband of Gomer the prostitute, personally and prophetically illustrates a marriage gone bad between God and unfaithful Israel. Chapter three of his prophecy lays out Israel's status after her religious restoration: she is in the house, but there is no intimacy, and there will generally be none until the latter days.

"For the children of Israel shall abide many days without king or prince, without sac-rifice or sacred pillar, without ephod or teraphim.

Afterward the children of Israel shall return and seek the Lord their God, and David their king. They shall fear the Lord and His goodness in the latter days" (Hosea 3:4,5).

The Church owes much to Israel,

"... to whom pertain the adoption, the glory, the covenants, the giving of the law, the service of God, and the promises; of whom are the fathers and from whom, according to the flesh, Christ came, who is over all, the eternally blessed God" (Romans 9:4,5).

Remember the confession of Jesus concerning His relationship to Israel:

"Now Jesus stood before the governor. And the governor asked Him, saying, 'Are you the king of the Jews?' Jesus said to Him, 'It is as you say'" (Matthew 27:11).

"I urge you in the sight of God who gives life to all things, and before Christ Jesus who witnessed the good confession before Pontius Pilate, to keep the commandment without spot, blameless until our Lord Jesus Christ's appearing, which He will manifest in His own time, He who is the blessed and only Potentate, the King of kings and Lord of lords, who alone has immortality, dwelling in inapproachable light, whom no man has seen or can see, to whom be honor and everlasting power. Amen" (1 Timothy 6:13-16).

These messages emphasize His sovereignty, the designation of King each time alluding to His Jewish, then universal Messiahship. Every truly Christian message has its roots in

Shadow and Substance

Israel's past, its trunk in her present, and its branches in her future. The true Church is the rose of her potential, and the fragrance of her portion. We complement each other in "the kingdom of God." Amen.

# Crest  Books

## The Salvation Army National Publications

Crest Books, a division of The Salvation Army's National Publications department, was established in 1997 so contemporary Salvationist voices could be captured and bound in enduring form for future generations, to serve as witnesses to the continuing force and mission of the Army.

## Christmas Through the Years
### A War Cry Treasury

Along with kettles and carols, the *Christmas War Cry* remains one of The Salvation Army's most enduring yuletide traditions. The anthology contains classics that have inspired *War Cry* readers over the past half century. Longtime subscribers will find this treasury to spark their memories, while those new to *The War Cry* will benefit from a rich literary heritage that continues to the present day.

## Celebrate the Feasts of the Lord
### The Christian Heritage of the Sacred Jewish Festivals
### by William W. Francis

This critically acclaimed book offers a fresh perspective on the sacred Jewish festivals, revealing their relevance to modern–day Christians. The work describes how Jesus participated in the feasts and how, in Himself, their meaning was fulfilled. Study questions at the end of each chapter make this book perfect for group or individual study.

## Never the Same Again
### Encouragement for new and not–so–new Christians
### by Shaw Clifton

This book explains the fundamentals and deeper aspects of faith in down–to–earth language, offering great encouragement and sound instruction. Whether readers are new Christians or revisiting the foundations of faith, the author helps them see that as they grow in Christ, they are *Never the Same Again*. An ideal gift for new converts.

## Pictures from the Word
### by Marlene J. Chase

This collection of 56 meditations brings to life the vivid metaphors of Scripture, addressing the frequent references to the vulnerability of man met by God's limitless and gracious provision. The author's writing illustrates passages often so familiar that their hidden meaning eludes us. *Pictures from the Word* will enrich your time of personal devotion and deepen your understanding of the Word.

## Romance & Dynamite
### Essays on Science and the Nature of Faith
#### by Lyell M. Rader

Whatever God makes works, and works to perfection. So does His plan for transforming anyone's life from a rat race to a rapture." Anecdotes and insights on the interplay between science and faith are found in this collection of essays by an "Order of the Founder" recipient known as one of The Salvation Army's most indefatigable evangelists.

## A Little Greatness
### by Joe Noland

Under the expert tutelage of author Joe Noland, readers explore the book of Acts, revealing the paradoxes of the life of a believer. Using word play and alliteration, Noland draws us into the story of the early Church while demonstrating the contemporary relevance of all that took place. A Bible study and discussion guide for each chapter allow us to apply each lesson, making this an ideal group study resource.

## Pen of Flame
### The Life and Poetry of Catherine Baird
#### by John C. Izzard with Henry Gariepy

Catherine Baird lived a life of extraordinary artistic value to The Salvation Army. As a poet, hymn writer, and editor, Baird changed the way the Army viewed the importance of the written word. From a decade of research and devotion John C. Izzard has painted a compelling word picture of one of the Army's strongest and yet most delicate authors.

## Easter Through the Years
### A War Cry Treasury

Spend time reflecting on the gift of salvation God has given by reading *Easter Through the Years,* a companion volume to *Christmas Through the Years.* Articles, fiction, poetry, and artwork culled from the last fifty years of the *Easter War Cry* will recount the passion of Christ and unveil the events surrounding the cross and the ways Easter intersects with life and faith today.

## Who Are These Salvationists?
### An Analysis for the 21st Century
#### by Shaw Clifton

A seminal study that explores The Salvation Army's roots, theology, and position in the body of believers, this book provides a definitive profile of the Army as an "authentic expression of classical Christianity." Salvationists and non–Salvationists alike will find this to be an illuminating look at the theology which drives the social action of its soldiers.

## Andy Miller
### A Legend and a Legacy
#### by Henry Gariepy

As an American Salvationist, Andy Miller has had a powerful spiritual impact on innumerable lives, both within and outside the ranks of The Salvation Army. His ministry across the nation has left its indelible impact upon countless people. Through anecdotes, this biography conveys the story of one of the most colorful and remarkable leaders in the Army's history.

## He Who Laughed First
### *Delighting in a Holy God*
### by Phil Needham

This invigorating book questions why there are so many sour–faced saints when the Christian life is meant to be joyful. Needham explores the secret to enduring joy, found by letting God make us holy to become who we are in Christ—saints. *He Who Laughed First* helps the reader discover the why and how of becoming a joyful, hilarious saint.

## Fractured Parables
### *And Other Tales to Lighten the Heart and Quicken the Spirit*
### by A. Kenneth Wilson

By applying truths of Scripture to contemporary situations, we find that people of the Bible are as real as we are today. Wilson illuminates beloved biblical accounts in a new light by recasting Jesus' parables in modern circumstances and language. He challenges as he entertains us, helping readers see the humor in the mundane while deftly showing the spiritual application.

## Our God Comes
### *And Will Not Be Silent*
### by Marlene J. Chase

Like the unstoppable ocean tide, God reveals Himself throughout all creation and will not be silent. The author shares in her poems the symmetry in all creation that draws us toward the goodness of God. She invites the reader to distinguish His voice that speaks as only our God can speak.

## A Salvationist Treasury
### *365 Devotional Meditations from the Classics to the Contemporary*
### edited by Henry Gariepy

This book brings to readers the devotional writings from over a century of Salvationists. From Army notables to the virtually unknown, from the classics to the contemporary, this treasure trove of 365 inspirational readings will enrich your life, and is certain to become a milestone compilation of Army literature.

## If Two Shall Agree
### *The Story of Paul A. Rader and Kay F. Rader of The Salvation Army*
### by Carroll Ferguson Hunt

The author tells the fascinating story of how God brought these two dedicated servants together and melded them into a compelling team who served for over 35 years, leading the Army to new heights of vision, ministry, and growth. Read how God leads surrendered believers to accomplish great things for Him.

## Slightly Off Center!
### Growth Principles to Thaw Frozen Paradigms
#### by Terry Camsey

Church health expert Terry Camsey seeks to thaw frozen paradigms of what is "Army." Challenging us to see things from a different perspective, he urges his readers to welcome a new generation of Salvationists whose methods may be different but whose hearts are wholly God's—and whose mission remains consistent with the principles William Booth established.

## The First Dysfunctional Family
### A Modern Guide to the Book of Genesis
#### by A. Kenneth Wilson

Bible families are just like ours—loving, caring, and as out of control and dysfunctional. In tracing the generations from Creation, Major A. Kenneth Wilson shows us how we may avoid our ancestors' mistakes in our family relationships. And through all of this dysfunctional rebellion, reconciliation, and return, readers will see that God is there, never giving up on us despite how badly we have treated Him and each other.

## Sanctified Sanity
### The Life and Teaching of Samuel Logan Brengle
#### by R. David Rightmire

Many Salvationists may still recognize the name, but fewer appreciate the influence that Brengle had on the development of the Army's holiness theology. Dr. Rightmire has written a theological reassessment of Brengle's life and thought to reacquaint those of the Wesleyan–holiness tradition in general, and The Salvation Army in particular, with the legacy of this holiness apostle.

## Turning Points
### How The Salvation Army Found a Different Path
#### by Allen Satterlee

Never in the history of the world has there ever been an organization like The Salvation Army. In *Turning Points,* Major Allen Satterlee outlines key moments in the history of the Army—including the combining of the ecclesiastical structure of the Christian Mission with the framework of the military, and the full frontal attack on society's ills waged by the Army in 1890—that continue to influence how Salvationists serve God and every generation faithfully.

## Leadership on the Axis of Change
### by Chick Yuill

In great demand as a conference and retreat speaker, Major Yuill describes today's Christian church as an institution that "faces great challenges stemming from inert cynicism within and dynamic changes without." Part manual on the functions and principles of leadership, part declaration of the need for change, this book serves all spiritual leaders with both provocation to action and direction toward success.

## Living Portraits Speaking Still
### A Collection of Bible Studies

Employing the art of compilation, Crest Books draws on established officer authors and contributors to *The War Cry* to examine the brilliance and vulnerabilities of the "saints of Scripture." *Living Portraits Speaking Still* groups eighteen Bible studies by theme, as a curator might display an artist's paintings. Each "gallery" focuses on a different aspect of God: Portraits of Sovereignty, Provision, Perfection, Redemption, and Holiness.

## A Word in Season
### A Collection of Short Stories

"For every season of our lives," writes Lt. Colonel Marlene Chase in her introduction, "the world of story can help us define our experience and move us beyond ourselves." More than thirty writers, including Max Lucado, have contributed to this compilation, which features factual accounts as well as fictional narratives within the panoply of Christian belief. They're the everyday experiences made extraordinary through faith.

---

*All titles by Crest Books can be purchased through your nearest Salvation Army Supplies and Purchasing department:*

ATLANTA, GA—(800) 786–7372
DES PLAINES, IL—(847) 294–2012
RANCHO PALOS VERDES, CA—(800) 937–8896
WEST NYACK, NY—(888) 488–4882